IMAGES OF MAN

IMAGES OF MAN
Essays on Philosophy and Religion

Samuel Umen

Philosophical Library
New York

Library of Congress Cataloging in Publication Data

Umen, Samuel.
    Images of man.

    1. Man.   2. Ethics.   3. Religion.   I. Title.
BD450.U455 1984   128   84-16653
ISBN 0-8022-2471-7

Published, 1985, by Philosophical Library, Inc.,
200 West 57 Street, New York, N.Y. 10019
Copyright 1984 by Samuel Umen
All rights reserved.
Manufactured in the United States of America

To
my sterling friends
Curtis L. Carlson
and
his beloved wife, Arleen

CONTENTS

Part II
RELIGION

Preface

Man's existence is sustained by bread; but it is ideas that give meaning to his life. Every great achievement in the world is the child of an idea. Without ideas civilization is inconceivable. Ideas are like flowers; some are annual and some are perennial. Some are meant only for a limited time and others are recrudescent; they persist through the ages.

It is the latter type of ideas that this book deals with. For example, ideas such as Freedom, Identity, Conscience, Mysticism, Morality, Religion, the State, Ethics, defy obsolescence. They are the lifeblood of every civilized society, man's undying concern.

Students of philosophy and religion will find the ideas discussed and analyzed in this volume helpful aids for their studies. The more perceptive layman too, after reading this book, will gain a deeper understanding of himself and the forces of life by which he is constantly shaped and influenced.

S.U.

Acknowledgments

To Dr. Robert E. Michael, Chairman of the English Department and Dean of Hawthorne College, I offer my deepest thanks for the honor he bestowed upon me by reading the manuscript and for his many helpful suggestions.

To Edward M. Shapiro, President of New Hampshire College, I am deeply indebted for the encouragement he gave me to have my manuscript, *Images of Man*, published.

To Jacqueline Hickox, the Humanities Secretary of New Hampshire College, I am most grateful for the many hours she devoted in painstakingly typing and proofreading the manuscript.

S.U.

Part I
PHILOSOPHY

At the moment when man's searching mind felt impelled to ask the question, independently of accepted tradition, as to the meaning of life and of the universe around us, then philosophy arose.

S.U.

1. The Uniqueness of Man

There are numerous definitions of man. Aristotle defined man as "by nature a civilized animal..." as "an animal capable of acquiring knowledge..." as "an animal that walks on two feet..." as "a political animal." In the *Eleventh Edition* of the Encyclopedia Britannica it says: "Man is a seeker after the greatest degree of comfort for the least necessary expenditure of energy." Protagoras maintained: "Man is the measure of all things." Scholastic philosophy accepted the definition of man as a rational animal. Do these definitions truly describe man?

In the last century vast efforts were made by biologists, physicists, psychologists, sociologists, and anthropologists to study and define man. Each definition given of him by the various sciences is incomplete, because each science deals with only a particular aspect of him. Even if all the definitions we have of man were combined, we would still lack a faithful portrayal of him. That so many attempts have been made to depict man indicates how difficult a task it is. It seems that an

3

exhaustive definition of a human being is not attainable. But what is there about a human being that renders the task of describing him comprehensively almost impossible? The difficulty, it appears, stems from the subject under scrutiny.

There are certain things about man that are revealed and certain things that are concealed. His physicality and functionality are clearly revealed and established. On the other hand, his innerness—that is, his potentiality—is locked up within him. As a natural being, he is determined by immutable principles. As a human being, he is unrestrained in his imagination and will.

Of all living beings on earth, the human being was created incomplete. The life of all other creatures is more or less predictable. It is not expected, for example, that an animal or bird will in the course of its existence become more of an animal or more of a bird. Concerning a human being, however, it is expected that he or she as time progresses will yet become more human. We think of man in terms of perfectibility. Unlike other living beings man is a process. He is always in a state of evolvement, in a state of flux. He is forever changing and transcending himself. There is no such entity as man in his final, permanent form. Man is rarely found in a definitive edition. Finality and humanity are mutually exclusive.

"One thing that sets man apart from animals," says Abraham J. Heschel, "is a boundless, unpredictable capacity for the development of an inner universe. There is more potentiality in his soul than in any other being known to us. Look at the infant and try to imagine the multitude of events it is going to engender. One child named Johann Sebastian Bach was charged with enough power to hold generations of men in his spell. But is there any potentiality to acclaim or any surprise to expect in a calf or colt? Indeed the enigma of human being is not what he is but what he is able to be."[1]

---

[1] Abraham J. Heschel, *Who Is Man?* (Stanford, Calif.: Stanford University Press, 1965), p. 39.

Man is different from every other being in creation and all men are different from each other. He is one of a kind. "Every man shall know and consider," said the Hasidic sage Rabbi Nahman of Bratzlav, "that in his qualities he is unique in the world and that none like him ever lived, for had there ever before him been someone like him, then he would not have needed to exist."[2]

Because man's innerness is not static and because each man is different, a general definition of him cannot be formulated. All that can be said of man is that he is in a continuous state of emergence.

The emergence of man does not occur automatically or naturally. While man is free to pursue and make real the image he projects of himself, free to choose what he wants to make of himself, free to realize his true self, to become what he is destined to be, he is also free to remain where he is at any point in his life or even imitate someone else's life. Man's emergence depends primarily on his will. But, before man becomes conscious of his freedom to make decisions concerning his life, he is already to a great extent fashioned and conditioned.

The influences of the environment on our existence are so numerous, penetrating, and subtle, that it is not always easy to determine which of the thoughts we think, convictions we hold, beliefs we proclaim and cling to are ours, and which are those of others we have at one time or another unconsciously absorbed.

Becoming what one is meant to be is an onerous task. It begins with a self-analysis, probing the inner recesses of one's being and discovering what of his way of life is truly his, arrived at by deliberate choice, and what of it is simply internalized commands. This is followed by an effort to liberate oneself from the hold "invisible others" of the past and present have on his life, and adopt a lifestyle which he can honestly call his own.

---

[2] Martin Buber, *Hasidism and Modern Man*, trans. by Maurice Friedman (Horizon Press, 1958), p. 111.

Self-liberation often means shedding old values and creating new ones, stepping out of the realm of inherited, time-honored practices no longer valid, and entering a new realm of behavior. Being uncertain of the consequences of such a move, few venture it. Most people prefer to remain as they are, to walk, so to speak, the trodden path.

The few stalwart spirits who in every generation choose to actualize their uniqueness, their potentialities, to pursue the goals of becoming what they were meant to be—they are our heroes. They are a blessing to themselves and to society. Through them, in the words of a Hebrew poet, "God renews His work of creation every day."

2. The Paradox Man

"The proper study of mankind," observed Alexander Pope, "is man." Pope was right in his observation. For there is no being in all creation that is more complex than man. He is the strongest being on earth and the weakest. "A vapor," remarks Blaise Pascal in his *Pensées*, "a drop of water suffices to kill him." He is the most ferocious of beings and, as the Psalmist has it, "he was made a little lower than the angels." He thinks the unthinkable, achieves the unbelievable, destroys his creations, and recreates them in an even more fascinating fashion.

Two opposite forces meet within him—an impulse for good and an impulse for evil. He is forever in conflict with himself. He sets for himself noble objectives and is driven to ignoble deeds. He longs for peace and makes war. He glorifies freedom and creates systems of enslavement. He prides himself on having a set of Laws from God to keep him on the path of righteousness, but more often than not forsakes it for the enticing promises made to him by the voice of evil. He sanctifies human life and does not hesitate to crush it as if it were a blight. He is compassionate, generous, loving, and forgiving, but also cruel, vengeful, selfish, and vindictive. On the one hand, he claims that his conduct is determined by inexorable laws of nature, by causes beyond his control; and on the other hand, he maintains that he is free to become what he wills, that his destiny is in his own hands. He warns himself that if he should forget the mistakes of his forebears, he will be destined to repeat them; yet, he willfully ignores his warning and is condemned to relive their woeful experiences.

In brief, man is the most paradoxical of paradoxes. He is an anomaly encased in an enigma. He is a bundle of contradictions.

Is there any basis for hope that this anomalous creature can become more human? In other words, is man improvable?

This question has been debated through the centuries. As a result, two conflicting views of him have emerged. One is pessimistic and the other optimistic.

The pessimists, it appears, arrive at their conclusion from a restrictive, one-sided view of the subject. They focus chiefly on man's evil and consider his nature as fixed—meaning that how he acts, how he lives, is merely a response to the demands of his nature. He has no power to control his manner of life, subdue the evil impulse which manages his every thought and act.

The English philosopher Thomas Hobbes, (1588-1679) a representative voice of the pessimists, describes man in his *Leviathan* as being in a "state of nature." He is aggressive, competitive, greedy, and antisocial, and "brutish." He desires only to outdo his fellow man; he mainly seeks gain and glory at the expense of another. Hobbes attacked the political philosophies of Plato and Aristotle for being unrealistic and for assuming wrongly that people were naturally capable of virtue and wisdom. Hobbes detected no sign by man's conduct that he will ever be any better than he is.

In every period and every place, one sees man's conduct repeating itself in its vilest form. Motivated by the instinct for survival, he lies, cheats, steals, robs, and kills. Even his occasional gesture of kindness extended to his brother man, the pessimists assert, is no more than a facade to beguile and target him as a means to an inhuman end.

The optimists, on the other hand, look at both sides of the human being and are encouraged. If history credits him with a great deal of cruelty, they indicate, it also takes note of his compassion; if it attributes much hatred to him, it does not overlook his expressions of love; if it charges him with measureless destructiveness, it also recognizes his incredible creativity.

The optimists deny that man's nature is so fixed that he cannot shape his future. They believe with the Italian Renaissance scholar Giovanni Pico della Mirandola, who in his *Oration on the Dignity of Man* has God saying to man: "A limited nature in other creatures is confined within the laws written down by Us. In conformity with thy free judgment, in whose hands I have placed thee, thou art confined by no bounds and thou wilt fix limits of nature for thyself.... Thou, like a judge appointed for being honorable, art the molder and maker of thyself; thou mayest sculpt thyself into whatsoever thou dost prefer."[3]

While it is true that in every generation an outcry for justice, freedom, human rights, and human dignity is sounded in the world, nevertheless, it is essential to understand, the optimists contend, that these concepts or ideals can never be realized in their fullness because they are fluid in their meaning. They expand in accordance with man's need, his level of consciousness. What is accepted by man as freedom or justice or human dignity in one period, is regarded by him as slavery, injustice, and indignity at a later time.

Man is dynamic, forever evolving, emerging. He is therefore never satisfied with conditions as he finds them. He is intent on

---

[3] Giovanni Pico della Mirandola, *Oration on the Dignity of Man*, trans. by A. Robert Caponigri (Chicago, 1956), pp. 4-5.

reaching higher goals, a greater, nobler degree of humanity. This tendency, the optimists maintain, is clearly shown by the institutions he establishes and re-establishes, the laws he enacts and reforms, the attitudes he adopts and changes toward every sphere of life. In all his attempts to improve his life, he simultaneously reaches a higher level of humanity.

The optimistic view of man receives much stronger support from his historical record than that of the pessimistic. Man has come a long way intellectually and spiritually since he first appeared on the stage of history.

"The conditions which make progress are very complex. The path goes like a mountain road, which turns upon itself in zigzag cuts or in spiral curves, so that even when you have ascended to a new height, you may seem to see before you substantially the same scenery as when you were on the parallel line below.... So mankind may behold some of the same disheartening human environment in London or New York as was seen in Babylon or Memphis. The prophets still denounce the same perennial iniquities. Can anyone doubt, however, that the word of the prophets now goes further, is more hopeful and intelligent, and addresses itself to an almost infinitely larger host of attentive hearers than in the days of Ramses or Xerxes?"[4]

---

[4]   Charles F. Dole, *The Ethics of Moral Progress* (New York: Thomas Y. Crowell and Co., 1909), p. 391.

3. How Humanism Views Man

The ancient saying that "there is nothing new under the sun" may not apply to the field of science, but it certainly is applicable to the realm of spiritual thought. There is hardly a spiritual idea which has come out of the mind of man in one period, that has not occurred to an individual or a group of individuals in a previous period. For example, Humanism, which appears as a new approach to life in our century, has been expressed in an informal way by a group of Greek philosophers as early as the fifth century before Christ. These philosophers, called the Sophists, were Humanists—for they turned their attention from cosmological speculation, which prevailed at that time, to the study of man.

The Humanism of the Sophists, a few centuries later, was swept away by Christianity, which by its teachings transferred man's attention entirely to things outside of and beyond himself. During the Middle Ages, as a result of the influence of Christian doctrine, this world was despised and men submitted to a vigorous discipline for eligibility in the world to come.

11

Nevertheless, due to the study of the old classics with their emphasis upon human personality and keen interest in this life, the Humanistic spirit in a small way was rekindled in the hearts and minds of some individuals who are described as the Renaissance Humanists. Even though the Renaissance Humanists failed in their attempt to popularize Humanism, they hastened the transforming of the medieval into the modern world.

Humanism is the name given to that ethical philosophy which embodies two special characteristics. First, it concentrates its fullest attention on the entire nature of man and all his latent possibilities. Second, Humanism views man as its center of reference instead of viewing him as a fragment of a larger whole, be it nature, God, or society. This does not necessarily mean that a Humanist lacks any cosmological beliefs. What it does mean is that for a way of life he depends upon his own intelligence in lieu of a transcendent force.

Humanism believes in the supreme worth of human life. Man, it stresses, stands on the highest rung in the creative process. He must therefore always be regarded as an end and never as a means to some other end, be it economic, political, or social.

Humanism is an attempt to comprehend human experience through human inquiry. All knowledge, it claims, is derived from this effort. It clings to the hope that as human knowledge increases, it will lead men to higher and greater levels of achievement. The primary interest of Humanism is human development. Even though the Humanist is aware of the limitations of human nature, his purpose, nevertheless, is to develop man's native talents to their highest degree. While Humanism recognizes the unequal capacities of human beings, and does not expect to develop all to the same degree of accomplishment, yet it insists upon developing each person to the utmost of his latent capacity.

Humanism accepts full responsibility for the condition of human life. The Humanist believes that practically all the evils in society have been caused by men themselves. The Humanist knows of no other source to turn to for the amelioration of the human condition but to himself. He assumes the responsibility for the hate, prejudice, envy, greed, cruelty, and poverty that are rife in the world. He knows that if human suffering is to be reduced and wherever possible eliminated, it is up to him to do it.

In brief, the Humanist envisions life as it might be upon this planet if all of man's intelligence is enlisted in its improvement. And he has faith that his vision of an improved life can be realized through man's own determination.

HUMANISM AND RELIGION

The religionist defines religion as knowing God and performing the duties that God expects of him. The Humanist, on the other hand, defines religion as knowing man and performing the duties toward him. Humanism does not negate the value of one's interest or desire to know God. Its emphasis, however, is on faith in man and man's duties towards his fellow man. The concentration in Humanism is not on the Eternal, the Most High, or the worship of Him, but on the problems with which man is beset. Humanism conceives of religion as spiritual enthusiasm directed toward the enhancement of the social order. Every faith, or part thereof, that ministers to this end is included in Humanism.

All Theistic religions are structured on the concept that there is a personal God at the center of all things from whom all power and blessings flow. Theistic religion urges man to bring himself into right relations with God—thus he will win God's favor. All the forms of worship, all types of rituals and sacraments are the result of man's attempts to attain the proper relationship with God and assure himself of God's blessings.

In opposition to this, the Humanists argue that it is futile for man to achieve a knowledge of God and bring himself into direct communion with Him by whatever means he employs. At its best, Theistic religion, say the Humanists, is speculative and has little influence on man's behavior toward his brother man. It is therefore more important for man, they continue, to bring himself into better relations with the portion of reality with which he is familiar, with which he comes into actual contact. This, they say, can be done by man's careful study of his environment, mastering himself, the forces about him, and using everything in his power for the enrichment of his own life and life as a whole.

Humanism regards religion as something more profound than mere belief in God. In its view, religion is far more than an effort to establish right relations with a Supernatural Being, but rather the impulse to elevate and ennoble human life. It is the striving for the fullest self-realization, and anything which leads to such fulfillment is, according to Humanism, religious—whether it be associated with the God concept or not.

HUMANISM AND ATHEISM

Because Humanism is hominocentric, instead of theocentric—that is, stressing the importance of man rather than God—it is often labeled as atheistic. Even though it is true that there are atheistic Humanists it is also true that Humanism is not identified with atheism. If by atheism one means the negation of a personal, transcendent God, then of course the Humanist would be considered as an atheist, but the term "atheist" properly used denies not only such an idea of God but the idea as an idea in itself. And while a Humanist is not a Theist, which involves belief in a guiding intelligence—working toward some definite end, he does not necessarily deny the possibility of the God idea. In fact, the Humanist's attitude is not that of denial at all, but that of inquiry. He is open-minded toward the idea of God, but his religion is not founded on such an uncertain idea.

THE POPULARITY OF HUMANISM

The appeal of Humanism in our day is very strong. It is continuously gaining ground. Every field of human thought and endeavor is affected by the Humanistic spirit. Practically all the branches of knowledge have become humanistic. In all the activities of life, except religion, people rely upon human experience for their knowledge. Only in religion do some still pretend to obtain knowledge from some supernatural source and depend upon it for guidance and help. Humanism is attempting to bring religion into line with the general trend of all human thought and endeavor, and thus make it a vital force in human life. The Humanists are working towards the integration of the scientific, social, and religious thought into one organized, unified philosophy that aspires to the best possible life for man.

CONCLUSION

Humanism views man as being the center and source of all the power that he requires for shaping his destiny, and for achieving the kind of life he wants for himself as an individual and for society as a whole.

4. How Existentialism Views Man

E xistentialism is a philosophy that has captured the imagination and aroused the interest, not only of professional philosophers in our day, but also of serious-minded students everywhere.

The widespread interest in Existentialism is due primarily to its relevance. The classical philosophies concentrate either on the impersonal world of Nature, on man in the abstract, on a transcendent Deity, or a depersonalized transcendent State. The concentration in Existentialism is completely on the life of the individual. It emphasizes the uniqueness and privacy of human existence, the inner, immediate experience of self-awareness, the individual as the instigator of action, the center of feeling, the existent in the whole range of his existing.

EXISTENTIALISM IS A PROTEST

Existentialism is a protest in the name of individuality. It is a revolt against mass movements which tend to crush and submerge the individual in the collective. It is a revolt against modern science and technology, which have reduced the individual to a thing and have rendered human life hollow and empty of meaning.

THEMES OF EXISTENTIALISM

A few of the themes with which Existentialism concerns itself are: freedom, responsibility, loneliness, decision, guilt, alienation, despair, finitude, and death. It is in the treatment and development of these themes drawn from the connate and affective elements in personal life that Existentialists have made their most important contribution.

Even though the ideas of Existentialism in one form or another can be found in ancient Judaism, in early Christianity, in the views of Socrates, in the writings of Kierkegaard, in Kafka's parables, and in Dostoevsky's novels, nevertheless, because of the present human condition, Existentialism's message has captured the attention of a large following in our day.

Never before has man felt more forlorn, abandoned, anguished, and confused than he does in our period. The culture which once guided man's life from the cradle to the grave, held people together, and gave purpose and meaning for their lives is fast deteriorating. It is no longer considered adequate. Man today is in search of a way of life that once again would help him face life. Any philosophy that would address itself directly to the individual and offer him guidance for his existence is bound to attract his interest. Existentialism claims to be such a philosophy.

EXISTENCE AND ESSENCE

The philosophy of Existentialism is predicated on the ideas of Existence and Essence. Concerning Existence, Existentialism limits it only to man. Though all beings in its view have existence in the sense that they have reality, they "stand out" from non-being, in actuality they simply are. They are what they are and they are always going to be what they have been. A plant, an animal, a stone, is simply a plant, an animal, a stone. They are just beings in their frozen staticity.

Man too "stands out" from non-being, but he also "stands out" from himself. He is the only being that has the possibility of transcending himself. Of him it cannot be said that what he is at any given time is what he will be tomorrow, the next day, or next year.

Man, unlike all other beings, is undetermined, always evolving, emerging, becoming. Existence, which is taken by the Existentialists in its root sense of "standing out" or "emerging," relates therefore only to man.

As for essence, that by which being is identified, Existentialism asserts that in almost every case the essence of being precedes its existence. In thinking, for example, of a chair, a house, a plant, an animal, its essence, its identity, is known before its appearance.

Only in one case, Existentialism holds, is the process reversed, does essence follow existence, and that case is man. Man's essence, owing to his ability to become something more than he is at any given time, cannot be known prior to his existence. And even after he comes into being, his essence remains unknown until he acts. In other words, man's essence is not given to him from the outside. He acquires it by the way he expresses his life, by the decisions he makes. It is decision, Karl Jasper maintains, that makes existence real. A man that makes no decisions has no existence. Of course there may be such a thing, but his being is the being of a thing, not the existence of a human being. A man who makes no decisions lacks personality because what he is, is determined for him from without. It can be said of him only what he is—not who he is—for he is nobody. In short, his essence precedes his existence. But to exist as a human being he must reverse his relationship; he must, that is to say, decide for himself what his life is to be.

Decision-making on the part of man implies freedom and freedom is linked with responsibility. Man's responsibility, according to Existentialism, is not exhausted by the act of choosing, but extends itself also to what is chosen; it lies in the consequences of the act and not just the act itself.

Man's responsibility begins with himself. He is responsible for his own individuality. But it does not end with him. As the Existentialists see it, man is responsible for more than what becomes of himself. He is also responsible for what becomes of others. In choosing for himself, he chooses for all men. In making a choice he is obliged to say, "This I choose, because that is what I would want chosen by mankind."

Existentialists universalize Kant's *Categorical Imperative*, which declares: "Act as if the maxim of thy action were to become by thy will a universal law of nature." This means that a person must never will what he cannot consistently will should be willed by all other rational beings. "It is wrong to lie, for in willing to lie you cannot consistently will that everyone else should always lie, or one's own lie would also be disbelieved; truth can do without falsehood but the lie cannot live without truth. In every choice I am responsible for the fate of mankind."[5]

Man's responsibility is greater than he imagines; it concerns mankind as a whole. By his conduct, man must bear in mind that he is creating an image of man—that in fashioning himself he is simultaneously fashioning man. When, for example, an individual commits himself to anything he is thereby deciding, legislating for all mankind.

But how can an individual know that he is the proper person to impose his judgment upon mankind? While there is nothing, say the Existentialists, to prove that one's decision is the cor-

[5] Abraham Kaplan, *The New World of Philosophy* (New York: Vintage Books, Random House, 1961), p. 108.

rect one, nevertheless, he must, before acting, imagine that the human race has its eyes fixed upon him and will regard his conduct as a guide for its own.

To be responsible for oneself causes much anguish; to be responsible for mankind causes greater anguish; but he who would be a man must accept the consequences of being one. All great leaders of men know anguish because of their responsibility to themselves and to others. To be human is to experience pain and anxiety.

So far, God, upon whom individuals depend for comfort, for promise in their moments of confusion, for help in their hours of vacillation, has not been referred to in our discussion of Existentialism. The reason for this is because many of the Existentialists are atheists and therefore do not concern themselves with God.

"Existentialism," says Sartre, "is not atheist in the sense that it would exhaust itself in demonstrations of the non-existence of God. Not that we believe God does exist, but we think that the real problem is not that of His existence; what man needs is to find himself again and to understand that nothing can save him from himself, not even a valid proof of the existence of God."[6]

In the view of a number of Existentialists, God's existence or non-existence has no effect on man's condition on earth. Thus they rule God out of existence and place the entire responsibility of the world in man's hands. With God's absence from the world, there is no determinism. Man is free. He has no reference to religious codes, to established scruples, to given formulae of right and wrong, to good and evil, to a particular set of values. In other words, "there is no *a priori* meaning of life, no value which, beforehand and in its own nature, is a value. Whatever meaning and value man can find in his life must be

---

[6] Walter Kaufman, *Existentialism from Dostoevsky to Sartre* (Cleveland and New York: Meridan, 1956), p. 311.

the outcome of his own choices, his own inventions...."[7] Without God, man is alone. He is left without excuses and is responsible for everything he does. He has no one to depend upon either within or outside of himself. Being so condemned, without help, without support, he is challenged to invent man.

Both the man who believes in God and the man who does not find themselves groping and confused. Both experience upheavals, repeated wars, industrial, political, and social difficulties. Man's salvation rests with man is the Existentialists' position. Simply stated, the world that man longs for, the heaven he dreams of, can be his only if he wills strongly enough to make it real.

In short, the Existentialists hold that each man must find purpose and direction for his own life, by his own decisions, his own goals. "Man is what he makes of himself," says Sartre.

If man is what he makes of himself, if what becomes of him is due to what he freely chooses to be, then it means that no one can ever do anything of any consequence for another. For if what one does for another is of importance to the beneficiary, to that extent he has lessened his existence; to that extent he has taken from his individuality, his authenticity.

"The highest relationship which can obtain between one man and another is that which was manifested in the life of Socrates. One can be a midwife to others, helping them give birth to themselves. A man cannot help others to achieve predetermined ends, and certainly not ends which he himself has predetermined, if those he would help are to exist as authentically human."[8]

CONCLUDING REMARKS

Existentialism focuses on the human condition. It graphi-

---

[7] Abraham Kaplan, *The New World of Philosophy*, p. 106.

[8] Ibid., p. 112.

cally depicts contemporary man in a state of loneliness, alienation and frustration. It pins the blame for man's plight on
Reason.

"The new philosophy of life, or Existentialism," writes Frederick Patka, "has been identified as the protest of life against
Reason. Reason has been made responsible for the universal
crisis of the modern man and modern life. The crisis is the
symptom of the overall alienation of man from himself, from
his fellow man, from his world and from his God."[9]

Reason, Existentialism contends, produced science and
technology, the effects of which are a technological economy
and industrialized society, with a loss of human identity and
the development of a one-sided human personality. Instead of
being master of that which man created with his intellect, he
ended up being enslaved by it. He is manipulated, directed, and
viewed by the captains of industry as a "thing" among things.

For man to transcend the situation by which he in entrapped,
Existentialism urges him to turn inward and resort to Intuition
as a guide for fashioning his life.

But, if man were to abandon Reason and rely solely on
Intuition as his source of knowledge, he would surely end up
being as one-sided as before. What he requires is both the use of
his intellect as well as intuition for a salubrious, balanced
existence.

Like all philosophies, Existentialism has its strong as well as
weak points. It is at its best in describing man's condition, in
awakening and raising his level of consciousness. In this
respect it has nobly succeeded and made a valuable contribution to Twentieth Century thought. Existentialism's weak spot
is the solution it prescribes for helping man to become master
of his destiny.

---

[9] Frederick Patka, *Existentialist Thinkers and Thought* (New York: Philosophical Library, 1962), pp. 52-53.

5. How Science Views Man

I n the tragedy *Prometheus Bound*, by Aeschylus, Prometheus is represented as the great lover of mankind. He found men existing wretchedly, like beasts in sunless caves, blindly ignorant and helplessly afraid. The instruments which could deliver them from this condition were in the hands of Zeus and the other gods; and the gods withheld their gifts. Prometheus stole fire from Olympus, brought it to man, and taught him the use of the arts and the powers of the civilized life. For this he was punished by the gods—chained to a lonely cliff, taunted and tortured for his presumption; but scornful and unyielding throughout the drama, he rises to a climax of defiance at the end, when brute forces of nature are unloosed upon him and he is swept down in a cataclysm of destruction.

Prometheus, in this play the champion of mankind, is generally understood to be a poetic figure standing for mankind itself, and the tragedy is regarded as the first great picture in literature of man fighting his way slowly and painfully in the teeth of a hostile world, forcing from a reluctant nature the secrets of his own well-being, and gradually subduing to his own purposes the brutish forces which once enslaved him and even threatened to destroy him.

Prometheus is regarded as a symbol of man's conquest of nature. He personifies the idea of scientific progress through human effort and sacrifice.

MAN IN THE FIELD OF SCIENCE

No one will deny that man's progress in the field of science has been phenomenal. If there is anything in the repertory of human activities and pursuits that has not proved to be a failure, it is precisely in this science, when one considers it circumscribed within its territory, nature. Within this realm, far from having failed, it has transcended all our hopes. Science has achieved things that irresponsible imaginings had never dreamed of.

Man is fully aware of the marvels and benefits of science, its triumph over nature. However, he is also becoming aware, more and more, that nature is only one dimension of human life and that the conquest of nature does not necessarily preclude failure with regard to the totality of human existence.

PHYSICAL SCIENCE AND HUMAN PROBLEMS

Physical science fails to furnish the solutions to human problems. Science has unlocked a host of nature's secrets; but it has failed to unfurl the mysteries of human nature. This is not to say that science completely excluded from its study the human being. But what it overlooked is the fact that human nature could not be treated in the same manner as nature, which it regarded as a thing.

NATURE IS A THING

Nature is a thing, a great thing, that is composed of many lesser things. Now, whatever be the differences between things, they all have one basic feature in common, which consists simply in the fact that things are, they have their being. And this signifies not only that they exist, that they are there, in front of us, but also that they possess a given, fixed structure or consistency. Given a stone, there exists forthwith, for all to see, what a stone is. The stone can never be something new and different. This consistency, given and fixed once and for all, is what we customarily understand when we speak of the being of a thing. An alternative expression is the word "nature." And the task of natural science is to penetrate beneath changing appearances to that permanent nature or texture.

When naturalist reason studies man it seeks, in consistence with itself, to reveal his nature. It observes that a man has a body, which is a thing, and hastens to submit it to physics; and since this body is also an organism, it hands it over to biology. It observes further that in man as in animals there functions a certain mechanism incorporeally, confusedly attached to the body, the psychic mechanism, which is also a thing, and entrusts its study to psychology, a natural science. But the fact is that this has been going on for three hundred years and that all the naturalist studies on man's body and soul put together have not been of the slightest use in throwing light on our most strictly human feelings, on what each individual calls his own life, that life which, intermingling with others, forms societies that in their turn, persisting, make up human destiny. The prodigious achievement of natural science in the direction of the knowledge of things contrasts brutally with the collapse of this same natural science when faced with the strictly human element.

HUMAN LIFE IS NOT A THING

Human life, it would appear then, is not a thing, has not a nature, and in consequence we must make up our minds to think of it in terms of categories and concepts that will be radically different from such as shed light on the phenomena of matter. Man, in a word, has not a nature; what he has is history. What nature is to a thing history is to man.

That man is not a thing to be studied from the outside as any other part of matter is further indicated by the *Kabbalists*, who had a sounder approach to the understanding of man than the scientists.

"Believe not," the *Zohar* exhorts, "that man consists solely of flesh, skin, bones, and veins. The real part of man is his soul, and the things just mentioned, the skin, flesh, bones, and veins, are only an outward covering, a veil, but are not the man."[10]

WHY WE THINK OF MAN HAVING A NATURE

The reason for our thinking of man as having or not having a nature is due to our ignoring the fact that man is a two-faceted being. He is both physical as well as spiritual in make-up. So, when we think of him in a biological sense, he of course has a nature. But when we consider him spiritually, we cannot attribute to him a nature—because spiritually he is unique. There are no two human beings who are alike. The nature of one cannot and will not be the same for the other. Spiritually speaking, then, we must conclude that it is impossible to universalize the nature of man.

---

[10] Adolphe Frank, *La Kabbala ou la philosophie des Hebreux* (Paris, 1843, German transl. by Adolph Jellineck), p. 76A.

6. How Man Views Himself in the Future

A prudent approach to life is to live on two levels—the practical and the theoretical. The practical level represents short-range goals—that is, satisfying immediate needs and desires. The theoretical level of life refers to long-range goals—that is, thinking and planning for the future.

It is essential to recognize that the theoretical aspect of life is as important as the practical. For the better we envision the future, the greater is the chance for our dreams to be realized.

At this point in time how do we regard the future? What plans do we have for it in the present that we may look forward to it with great expectations?

In his book *The State of the Siege*, C.P. Snow says that, after traveling many thousands of miles around the world, he returned with "one overmastering impression"—that nearly everyone he talked with was worried about the future—that

27

people were turning inward and were afraid that we were headed toward major catastrophes of unprecedented nature.

Karl Jasper's view of our moment of history is similar to what C.P. Snow had picked up in his discussions with people during his travels around the world. "The mental situation in our day," Jasper observes, "is pregnant with possibilities; and it is one which, if we are inadequate to the tasks which await us, will herald the failure of mankind."[11]

What are the causes for man's dim view of the future? There are numerous reasons for his despondency and bewilderment concerning the years ahead. Among the many reasons for his pessimistic outlook, in my estimation, there are three basic ones. These are: (1) the many rapid changes that have occurred in the last half century, (2) the lag in our thinking in dealing with the problems that change has wrought, and (3) the breakdown in our value system.

In past centuries changes occurred slowly over a long period of time. Society was able to absorb the effect of the changes with little or no disturbance. Now, radical, multitudinous changes come within the life span of individuals. This creates myriad problems not only for individuals but for society as a whole and its institutions. Our century has witnessed scientific and technological changes as great as or even greater than those which appeared during the past two thousand years. Within a few generations we have changed from a society predominately rural to a highly industrialized machine civilization that is becoming increasingly complex, interdependent, and impersonal.

Before we had become adjusted to the industrial and technological revolutions of the nineteenth century, we were ushered into the age of electronics, computers, automation, cybernetics, mass media, the knowledge explosion, the population explosion, the thermonuclear age, and the space age. As a

---

[11] Karl Jasper, *Man in the Modern Age*, trans. by Eden and Cedar Paul (New York: Doubleday, Anchor Books, 1951), p. 159.

result of all this, people feel disoriented, confused, maladjusted. They do not know what to expect next and how to plan their lives.

The second reason why people look at the future with hesitancy, doubt, and despair is because there is a lag in our thinking. Our problems are new and global and we approach them with outdated thought. Our concepts are still essentially local, regional, tribal, and nationalistic. This is not a matter of irrelevant patriotism, for realistic loyalties promote cohesive bonds and foster shared visions and goals. It is rather that aristocentric myths prevent an accurate understanding of the nature of the global problems which threaten us and make it impossible to set in motion the forces that would be effective against the large-scale problems we face. Sometime before his death, Albert Einstein, who has had much to do with bringing in the age we are grappling with, said: "The unleashed power of the atom has changed everything except our way of thinking. Thus we are drifting toward a catastrophe beyond comparison. We shall require substantially a new manner of thinking if mankind is to survive."

The third basic cause for our fear of the future is due to the breakdown of our value system. This has given rise to a welter of conflicting values that render us powerless in making the right decisions and acting upon them. Where there are no objective standards, it is hard to criticize or condemn anyone for his or her behavior. The line between right and wrong is erased.

Our value system developed in a simple agricultural society that was relatively static. Today we live in a complex mechanized civilization with scores of new ways of injuring, killing, lying, and stealing. Our failure to bring our morals up to date and apply them to our society is one of the major causes of the crisis we face—one of the reasons for our depressed state of mind and fear of the future.

"With all that and all that," as the poet Robert Burns would say it, we dare not give up hope. Man, after all, is unpredictable. He has demonstrated time and again in his long history on earth that he can think the unthinkable and achieve the unbelievable. His genius has not run its course.

"Man," says Karl Jaspers, "is always something more than what he knows of himself. He is not what he is simply once for all, but is a process, he is not merely an extant life, but is, within that life, endowed with possibilities through the freedom he possesses to make of himself what he will by the activities on which he decides."[12]

Though the present looks dark and threatening, and the future even more so, yet we must act wisely and trust that generations after us will praise us for the kind of world we have fashioned for them.

---

[12] *Ibid.*, pp. 22-23.

7. The Forces by Which Man Is Shaped

The life history of a human being is traceable to generations of men which preceded him. His life is connected with the lives of others which flow into his. His thoughts, his acts, his feelings, all these are the outcome of what his predecessors felt and did. It is transmitted to him from their lives and their blood and from their social milieu. His body begins with a single cell, and is formed by a union of cells emanating from the bodies of his ancestors of a remote age. This is the hereditary channel of his life. The special kind of cells in which heredity is conveyed to him is known as the germ-plasm. It is the source of the dispositions, capacity, potentialities, physical tendencies that each person has at birth.

The environmental or social influences reach him through association with others, through the speech he learns from his family, which it acquired from its elders, and thus going back to the earliest history of the human race or even to a prehuman period. The same is true of the use of tools, the mastery of the arts, and whatever else one learns. All this is one's social heritage from an ancient past. In brief, man is the product of two forces, heredity and environment.

Heredity is the chief source for his bodily traits. The child of a dark race will be dark no matter in what society he grows up, and will also have the hair, the shape of head, the height, and all the peculiarities of the racial type from which he received his germ-plasm. A child of feeble-minded ancestors or ancestors of unusual ability is apt to resemble them. Heredity is not only responsible for the child's definite physical development, but also his aptitude, disposition, and all other physical tendencies that all of us are born with.

From his environment he receives the motivation, stimulation, and teaching by which his capacities, tendencies, and talents are helped to develop. It gives him a particular language and one special set of ideas or outlook, rather than another—such as loving the country in which he lives rather than some other country.

CAN HEREDITY BE ALTERED?

It is often asked whether our mode of life can alter heredity. For example, suppose I devote myself to study, will this in any way affect the germ-plasm of my offspring so that their mental capacities will be increased? The prevailing scientific answer is that it does not. By the same token, it is not expected that an athlete will have stronger children because of his training.

Despite much research on the matter, it has not yet been proven that "acquired traits"—that is, those due to a particular mode of life—are transmittable through the germ-plasm. This theory being correct, and we have no evidence to think otherwise, it must not be assumed that ameliorating the mental condition of parents, or bettering their physical lives in any way, will in the slightest manner improve the hereditary factor in their future children.

CAN HEREDITY BE INFLUENCED?

It is the belief of some biologists that while one's mode of life can have no direct effect upon heredity, yet it can be influenced indirectly by the process known as Selection. This is based upon the fact that the germ-plasm carried by one individual may differ considerably from that carried by another, even in the same family, and varies widely as between different families, and still more widely as between different races—although all may have remotely a common ancestry. If, then, we know what sort of germ-plasm a certain individual or family or race carries, and can increase or decrease the number of children inheriting it, we can change, more or less, the proportion which this kind of heredity bears to other kinds.

Starting, for example, with a mixed population and being able to control mating and the number of children, it would be possible in this way to breed people who are dark or light, tall or short, blue-eyed or black-eyed, bright or dull, and thus increase or diminish any hereditary trait ascertainable enough to be made the basis of selection.

THE RELATION BETWEEN HEREDITY AND ENVIRONMENT

Since the two forces, heredity and environment, are derived from two separate and different sources, one would imagine that it would be easy to determine which of his thoughts and acts are attributable to one or the other force. Unfortunately, this cannot be done. For when our individual life begins, the two elements, the hereditary and the social, merge in a new whole and cease to exist as distinct and separable forces. Nothing that the individual is or does can be ascribed to either alone, because everything is based on habits and experiences in which the two are inextricably intermingled. As a matter of fact, the two elements as applied to the life of a human being are abstractions; the real thing is a total organic process not separable into parts.

WHICH IS MORE IMPORTANT, HEREDITY OR ENVIRONMENT?

It is sometimes asked which of the two elements are more important. We might as well ask which is the more important member of the family, the father or the mother. The question on the surface seems rather silly. Both are equally important, since each is indispensable and their functions, being different in kind, cannot be properly measured. But if both are equally important, then a consideration of the relation between heredity and environment becomes valueless. This is not necessarily so. The fact is that, although it is plain that they are, in general, complementary and mutually dependent, we usually do not know precisely what the contribution is of each in a given case, and so may be in doubt whether to seek improvement by working on the germ-plasm or through social influence. It is only with reference to general theory that the question of which is more important is silly. With reference to a specific problem it may be quite pertinent—just as it might be quite pertinent as regards to the troubles of a specific family to discover whether you could best reach them through the father or through the mother. And while direct measurement of the factors, at least where the mind is involved, is impossible, since they have no separate existence, there may be roundabout methods of inference which shed some light upon the matter.

Many race questions are of this sort. There are, for example, differences between the Occidental and the Oriental peoples, such as language, religion, and moral standards. These differences and difficulties are purely social and are alterable through education. On the other hand, color, stature, and shape of eyes are definitely hereditary and are unchangeable by education. These differences in themselves may not be too important. But there are also such subtle differences as temperament, mental capacity, and emotional gifts which hinder peaceful relations among the races or make one feel superior to the other. As yet, we do not know how to treat these problems, but it is vital that we should.

If we could find the answers to these questions, we would simultaneously be able to attack a host of other problems with which society is plagued. With reference to criminals, we don't know whether in certain cases education or the prevention of propagation is the proper deterrent. Again, with reference to men of genius, is education the method to be employed for developing more of them or are we to follow the advice of Sir Francis Galton (1822-1911), the founder of eugenics, who held that above all things men of great ability are to be induced to have more children? Until we find the proper answers to questions of this kind, we cannot be too successful in bettering the course of human life.

8. The Way to Self-Discovery

E very person in the world represents something new, something that never existed before, something original and unique. It is therefore every individual's foremost task to actualize his unprecedented, never-recurring uniqueness.

Through self-actualization a person discovers his identity, who he really is. Actually, each person has two identities. One is outer and the other is inner. These are often confused. One's outer identity is established by his name, physical appearance, and his family background. The inner identity of a human being, because it is inner, is not so easily discernible. It is hidden within him; it refers to his uniqueness, which he personally needs to discover and actualize if he is ever to know himself.

Having fathomed the vast difference between the outer and

inner identity of an individual, a Hasidic Rabbi once remarked, "If I am I only because you are you, and you are you only because I am I, then I am not I and you are not you." The Rabbi's subtle remark stresses the point that it is not by our outer marks that we are properly differentiated from one another, but by our special characteristics and singular gifts.

Now, if it is true that a human being is born with a particular endowment which he and no other possesses, why is he not aware of it? Why must he discover it? The reason for this is because man never knows about himself until he is tried and tested in the crucible of life. By his actions, by his decisions and choices, his precious something is revealed to him.

The process of self-discovery is a trying one and the task of self-actualization is fraught with difficulty. For our early thoughts, beliefs, feelings, are by no means distinctively ours. They are imparted to us by our parents, teachers, the community, our surroundings. From our very birth practically, we are indoctrinated, directed, and conditioned by forces from the outside. We are what others have made of us. We are not ourselves.

However, he who is in search of his true self, breaks out of the mold in which he was set, examines the life that was imposed upon him, and refashions it in accordance with the strongest promptings of his heart and mind. By pursuing this course, he thinks his own thoughts, espouses causes he is drawn to, takes positions on matters close to his heart, and is fully prepared to suffer the consequences for his behavior regardless of what they might be.

Because self-discovery and self-actualization call for determination, courage, and effort, most people avoid this venture. They dread the thought of acting freely and independently. They fear that their independence might alienate them from loved ones, friends, and neighbors. Hence they choose to be as they are, as the external influences have made them. On the other hand, some who long to realize their potentiality but lack the courage to do so, resort to imitating figures who are admired and respected. These imitators eventually learn that by assuming another's role, they are neither themselves nor like the ones whom they imitate. The price for their deception is guilt, anxiety, and despair.

Few men have perceived as profoundly the effects of imitating the life of another, or hiding in the crowd to escape the responsibility for one's own existence, as did the Danish philosopher Søren Kierkegaard. With keen psychological insight, he points out that the most common despair results from not choosing or willing to be one's self, and that the deepest form of despair comes from choosing to be other than one's self. On the other hand, to will to be that self which one truly is is indeed the opposite of despair, and this choice is the highest responsibility of man.

Those who eschew the responsibility of self-realization and hide in the crowd, Kierkegaard urges them to consider that "a crowd...in its very concept is the untruth by reason of the fact that it renders the individual completely impenitent and irresponsible." "The crowd," he says, "is composed of individuals: it must therefore be in every man's power to become what he is, an individual. From becoming an individual no one, no one at all, is excluded except he who excludes himself by becoming a crowd.... If I were to desire an inscription for my tombstone, I should desire none other than 'That Individual.' "[13]

The epitaph "That Individual" represents the person who actualized his unprecedented, never-recurring uniqueness. Were this man an artist, his style was new and invigorating; were he a literary figure, he opened our eyes to an area of life that was hitherto hidden from us; were he a philosopher, he introduced a concept that shed fresh light on the meaning of our existence; were he a craftsman, he indicated a way of performing his line of work more skillfully and more efficiently.

---

[13] See section on Kierkegaard in Walter Kaufman, ed., *Existentialism from Dostoevsky to Sartre* (New York: World Publishing, 1956), pp. 98-99.

The treasures that are society's pride are no other than the expressions of "That Individual." He is its creative force. It is through his contribution that our lives are enriched and ennobled.

9. Life's Purpose

Man lives in two worlds. One is that of Reality and the other is that of Ideality. The world of Reality is that of man's everyday experiences. In this world, man's lot is toil, sweat, tension, pain, suffering, disillusionment, and disappointment. From these experiences no one is exempt. If there are some who appear favored, they are not without fear and anxiety which afflict and oppress them.

"Unless suffering is the direct and immediate object of life," says Arthur Schopenhauer, "our existence must entirely fail of its aim."[14]

Were it not for the world of Ideality, man could not survive. He is preserved by escaping from time to time into this world.

---

[14] Arthur Schopenhauer, *Essay on the Sufferings of the World*, trans. by T. Bailey Saunders (New York: Willey Book Co.), p. 1.

Here he finds a modicum of relief. Here his bruised and wounded soul is soothed and healed. In this world he is given hope and promise. In this world he hears the comforting words that his strain and stress are not in vain. His struggle with himself will produce a better man. His battle outside of himself will create a better society of men. A day is coming when "Nation shall not lift up sword against nation.... The wolf shall dwell with the lamb.... The earth shall be full of the knowledge of the Lord as the waters cover the sea." (Isaiah 2:4; 11:9.)

In brief, the world of Ideality is the source of man's energy, the source of his dreams and visions, the driving force behind all his acts.

With the approach of every New Year, we are afforded a glimpse of how man steps out for a moment from the Real world and enters the world of Ideality. His faith at this time is at its peak. He believes with Robert Browning that "the best is yet to be," that whatever the old year withheld from him, the New Year will deliver. Thus he is refreshed, invigorated, and directs his gaze toward new horizons. His heart is filled with renewed courage and confidence.

As the curtain slowly rises on the New Year, he observes that there is hardly a noticeable difference between the days of the old year and those of the new. He is puzzled, perplexed, and asks: "Will the good that I anticipate ever be realized? Is there meaning to all that I am doing? Does life truly have any purpose? Could it be that King Solomon was right when he exclaimed: 'Vanity of vanities all is vanity'?" (Ecclesiastes 1:1.)

The question concerning man's suffering and the meaning of his life has engaged the minds of thoughtful men throughout history. They found the answer to the question to be man himself. In observing him carefully, they noticed that man reveals himself at his best while he is in the process of attaining rather than in attainment; in his pursuit of goals rather than in the realization of them.

"Need and struggle," says William James, "are what excite

and inspire us; our hour of triumph is what brings the void. Not the Jews of the captivity, but those of the days of Solomon's glory are those from whom the pessimistic utterances in our Bible come. Germany, when she lay trampled beneath the hoofs of Bonaparte's troops, produced perhaps the most optimistic and idealistic literature that the world has seen; and not till the French 'milliards' were distributed after 1871 did pessimism overrun the country.... The history of our own race is one long commentary on the cheerfulness that comes with fighting ills."[15]

What William James is saying, and he is not alone in his view, is that the meaning of life's travails and life's purpose manifests itself not in tasks done no matter how rewarding, but in tasks yet to be undertaken, not in challenges met, but those to be met, not in dreams realized, but in laboring toward those that are yet to be fulfilled.

Life's purpose is action. This truism is more aptly expressed by Fyodor Dostoevsky in his *Notes from Underground*.

"Man," says Dostoevsky, "likes to make roads and to create, that is a fact beyond dispute. But why has he such a passionate love for destruction and chaos also?.... May it not be that he loves chaos and destruction because he is instinctively afraid of attaining his object and completing the edifice he is constructing? Man is a frivolous and incongruous creature, and perhaps, like the chess player, loves the process of the game, not the end of it...perhaps the only goal on earth to which mankind is striving lies in this incessant process of attaining...not in the thing to be attained..."[16]

The notion that life's purpose is found in attaining rather than in attainment had been entertained long ago by the bibli-

---

[15] William James, *Essays on Faith and Morals* (New York: Longman's Green and Co., 1947), p. 16.

[16] Fyodor Dostoevsky *Notes from Underground*, Walter Kaufman, ed. *Existentialism from Dostoevsky to Sartre* (New York: World Publishing, 1956), p. 77.

cal author of the *Book of Genesis* in the story of the Garden of Eden.

Adam, according to the story, is placed in the Garden and is provided with every conceivable need. In addition, he is promised eternal life if he would only honor one simple command— not to eat of the fruit of one tree in the Garden, "The Tree of Knowledge." Should he fall prey to temptation and disobey the one command, he is clearly warned that he would forfeit all his privileges, be driven from the Garden, and be consigned to a life of struggle and eventual death.

Despite our expectation, Adam ignores the command and exchanges all that is given and promised him for a limited span on earth studded with trial, frustration, sweat, and tears. Why does Adam behave in what appears so strange and senseless a manner?

Using Adam as a symbol for man, and the Garden as a symbol for attainment, the writer essays to indicate that attainment equates with boredom and emptiness; that to experience himself, man needs worlds to conquer, mysteries to unlock, mountain peaks to climb, visions to be inspired by, goals to work for; that to long and strive for paradise is more rewarding, more exciting for him than attaining it. Thus, he chooses a brief life of toil ending in death, over an interminable existence with every aspiration fulfilled and nothing to look forward to.

10. On the Unreality of Time

Of all the concepts that test the human mind there is no other that is as difficult to comprehend as the concept of time. "It is impossible to meditate on time and the mystery of the creative passage of nature," said Alfred North Whitehead, "without overwhelming emotion at the limitation of human intelligence."[17]

"What is time? If no one asks me," said St. Augustine, "I know. If I try to explain it to someone asking me, I don't know."[18]

---

[17] See "Past/Present/Future" by James L. Christian in *Philosophy on Introduction to the Art of Wondering* (New York: Holt, Rinehart and Winston, 1977) Chapter 4-2, p. 257

[18] St. Augustine, *Confessions*, Book XI, trans. Dr. E.B. Pussey (London: 1907).

HOW WE REFER TO TIME

In our daily speech we refer to time in a variety of ways. We say, for example, that time flies; we thereby ascribe to it the characteristic of motion. Time, we say, heals; thus we attribute to it some kind of magical power. Most often we think of time as a measuring device. This or that task, we say, will take so many years, months, weeks, days, or hours to complete. By dividing time into units small or large, we seem to view it as a substance.

The truth of the matter is that time in actuality is unreal. All our references to it are simple expressions of convenience. Time as such is unmeasurable, unmoving, and indivisible. It has neither beginning nor end. It is synonymous with eternity.

But if time does not move and is indivisible, how did man arrive at the contrary notion of it? It seems that man's idea of time—that is, as he ordinarily regards it—has come to him from observing light and darkness, day and night, and also the change of seasons.

In reality, time represents the continuous mutations that are occurring within man and his environment.

The past is identified in his mind by unforgettable events. The present he equates with ongoing activities through him and through others. The future he relates to plans and programs awaiting his hand.

Time in the abstract, by itself is inconceivable, incomprehensible, empty of meaning, and cannot be recalled. Only happenings are remembered or recalled.

As soon as one stops thinking of events, time loses its meaning, becomes completely unfathomable, and disappears from the mind.

Time, according to Henri Bergson, is commonly conceived of abstractly and is thought of as composed of discrete instants or moments which follow one another in a uniform manner. For the purposes of science, such an abstraction is often necessary. But real time as it actually passes, as it is actually experienced and lived in the world of changing events, is not composed of such instants which replace one another. It is duration—that is, a continuous change in which "the past gnaws into the future and swells as it advances."[19]

When time is conceived of as a succession of discrete parts, it is incomprehensible how any period of time—say, an hour—can ever elapse, since it involves the sequence of an infinity of parts. Real time is only apprehended in intuition and is continuous duration. The abstract concept of time, according to Bergson, as it is commonly used in science, is the result of an attempt to assimilate it to Space, or at least to measure it by means of certain correlated positions in Space.

---

[19] H. Bergson, *Creative Evolution* (New York: Holt, Rinehart and Winston, 1911), p. 5.

11. Past and Present—Present and Future

W hy should we be concerned with the past? In what way, if any, does it have any connection with our present existence? The present, it is often heard said, is the only time that has any meaning for us, it is the only time that we are really conscious of. It represents our thoughts, feelings, acts, involvements, and our goals. It is our life as we know it and live it.

Besides, life is dynamic, forever changing. Conditions and circumstances are different for each succeeding generation. What is there then that we can learn from the past? The past is a time that is gone, done with. It cannot be dealt with. It remains irreversible. Neither the good it records nor its evil can have any effect upon the present moment. Preoccupying ourselves with the past is no more than a futile exercise.

Even though the past appears to be completely behind us

and in no way relates to the present, yet, as soon as one asks the question "Who am I?" he cannot attempt an answer without referring to the past. To discover who one is, he has to turn back the pages of his life. It is only by peering into all his yesterdays, all his yesteryears, that he will be afforded an inkling as to who he is.

One's background, the environment in which he grew up, the experiences he had, the challenges he faced, the influences that played upon him from his surroundings—all these are one's past and shed light on his identity. It explains to a great extent how he came to be who he is. After all, how he lives, the life style he pursues, the beliefs he clings to, the values he cherishes, did not spring up in him spontaneously. These are his past, expressing itself through him now—in the present. Hence, the answer to the question who one is can only be given with the aid of his past.

The notion that the past is wholly detached from the present is utterly false. The truth is that there is no real line of demarcation between the two tenses. The past, properly viewed, flows into the present. We are what we are and who we are by virtue of the past. Whatever great achievements we boast of and claim credit for in the present, are merely extensions and improvements of what we inherited from the past. Each generation adds of its own genius to what was produced by prior generations.

Nothing in the present can be fully fathomed without the light of the past. This is true of individuals as well as of nations.

PRESENT AND FUTURE

Now what about the future? Does it have any connection with the present? What linkage can there be between a time that is here and a time yet unborn?

As it appears to the unthinking that the past and present are apart from each other, so it also appears to them that there is a gulf between the present and the future.

Although the future seems to be a distance away from the present, in actuality the present is the future in the making. It represents our dreams, our hopes, imaginings, objectives, that which we want from ourselves and for ourselves.

Man is driven by a desire to know more, to create newer and more wondrous things, to be happier than he is, to reach, so to speak, the "land flowing with milk and honey."

Man is never content with his achievements. He is relentlessly striving to attain, but attainment leaves him dissatisfied. If it were not so, he would still be at the edge of the cave whence civilization started on its endless march forward.

Thus, everything man does, all his thoughts and aspirations are related to a coming day, coming year, the future. The tasks he begins in the present, he hopes to be rewarded for tomorrow or the next day.

The future is the source of his strength, inspiration, and motivation. His concentration on it makes the anxieties and insecurities from which he suffers in the present more bearable. Without a dream in his heart for a brighter day, his present would lose its meaning for him and his life would be more sorrowful than it is.

Even though the future is hidden from our eyes, much of what it has to reveal depends upon what we do in the present. In large measure, the future is in our hands; we are its shaper, definer, and fashioner.

The problems by which we are beset in the present and which we fail to solve, will inevitably come to haunt us in the future. As the old adage warns us: "They who sow the wind shall reap the whirlwind." The future is very much intertwined with the present.

In sum, there is no gap between the past and the present as well as the present and the future. The break between them are mere conjurations of the mind.

12. The Value of Conformity and Nonconformity

CONFORMITY DEFINED

Conformity may be defined as the endeavor to maintain the standard established by a group. It is a voluntary imitation of modes of conduct, concerning itself for the most part with what is outward and formal.

WHY PEOPLE CONFORM

Man is the product of his environment. This means that at birth he is a *tabula rasa*, and that the impressions which his mind receives from the members of his family, community, and nation are largely responsible for his conduct, his education, his beliefs, his life's objectives, ideals, hopes, and aspirations. What one takes from his environment is regarded by him as true, good, and proper. It is seldom evaluated, questioned, or compared with what others from another environment claim to be good, true, and proper. But suppose a person should

50

begin to doubt the value of the standards by which he was fashioned, and suppose the thought should occur to him to abandon the accepted standard and adopt one more to his satisfaction. He would then have to reconcile himself to the idea of being rejected by the members of his family, his community, and his nation.

While some may be prepared to suffer the pain of rejection, most prefer to remain accepted. Conformity, then, is motivated first by the system of life to which we are inured from birth onward, and secondly by the fear of becoming the target for ridicule. Loneliness is fearsome and depressing and nonconformity condemns us to it.

We all cherish our ideas, our manners, our beliefs, everything by which we were nurtured and fashioned, and anything that breaks in upon it is annoying to us and evokes our resentment. We feel most at home with those who are like ourselves, those who are of the same environmental stamp. So, our first tendency is to suppress the peculiar, and we endure it only if we must.

Thus every variant idea of conduct has to fight its way for acceptance. As soon as anyone attempts to do anything unexpected, as soon as one introduces an unfamiliar thought, he is sneered at, shoved, coaxed, and forced back into the rut.

There are no people who are altogether nonconformers, or who are completely tolerant of nonconformity in others. Even the innovator is nearly as apt as anyone else to decry innovation by others.

THE VALUE OF CONFORMITY

While conformity seems to stand in the way of progress, yet it is not without value. For the standards which it presses upon the individual are the valuable products of cumulative thought and experience of the past, and with all their limitations and imperfections serve as an indispensable foundation of life. "It is said with truth that conformity is a drag upon genius; but it is equally true and important that its general action upon human nature is elevating. We get by it the selected and systemized outcome of the past, and to be brought up to its standards is a brief recapitulation of social development; it sometimes levels down but more generally levels up."[20]

WHY SOME PEOPLE DO NOT CONFORM

Though it is true that most people conform to the standards which they inherit and are not inclined to think about their relevance, significance, and particularly their original purpose, still, there are a few in every age who feel impelled by the demand of circumstances to question the validity of the standards to which they are expected to conform and who, upon finding them outdated and irrelevant, break away from these accepted standards and regardless of consequences proclaim their own—which are more in keeping with the new conditions of life. Until such time as the new standards win the approval of the masses, the innovators are regarded as queer, disloyal, disrupters of the good life, social pariahs, and nonconformers.

Just as the majority of people find security and serenity in conformity, so there is a minority who experience the true joy of living through nonconformity. To brave the disapproval of men is a tonic to the nonconformist. He feels himself to be a cause. He discovers purpose and meaning to his life. He hears the sound of applause from the nonconformists of all ages, as he takes his stand on the issue which seems to him to be vital.

Nonconformity is characteristic of the more energetic states of the human mind. Men of great vigor are sure to be nonconformers in some important respect. "Men are conservatives when they are least vigorous, or when they are most luxurious. They are conservatives after dinner, or before taking their rest;

[20] Charles H. Cooley, *Human Nature and the Social Order* (New York: Charles Scribner's Sons, 1922), p. 297.

when they are sick or aged. In the morning, or when their intellect or their conscience has been aroused, when they hear music, or when they read poetry, they are radicals."[21]

A RATIONAL ATTITUDE TOWARD CONFORMITY AND NONCONFORMITY

A sound, rational attitude toward the question of conformity and nonconformity for one's own life ought to be: speak your thoughts, assert your individuality, in matters which you deem important; conform in those which are of small consequence. To choose a conspicuously individual way of doing everything is well-nigh impossible to a healthy-minded person, and to attempt it would redound to one's self-injury, as one would be closing the channels of communication and sympathy through which he partakes of the life around him. It is wise for a person to preserve his energy for matters in regard to which persistent conviction impels him to insist upon his own way.

Society requires a proper balance of stability and change, uniformity and differentiation. Conformity is the phase of stability and uniformity, while nonconformity is the phase of differentiation and change. While change does not introduce anything wholly new, it does, however, effect the reorganization of existing material which results in the transformation and renewal of human life.

---

[21] Ralph Waldo Emerson, Address on New England Reformers, First Edition. (New York: Wm. H. Wise and Co. Publishers, 1929).

13. Education and Democracy

THE FUNCTION OF EDUCATION

The term education is derived from the Latin root *e-ducere*, which means "to bring out or lead out." Education then means the bringing out and developing of an individual's capacity for life.

"Sound education," said John H. Pestalozzi, "stands before me symbolized by a tree planted near fertilizing waters. A little seed, which contains the design of the tree, its form, and proportions, is placed in the soil. See how it germinates and expands into trunk, branches, leaves, flowers, and fruit! The whole tree is an uninterrupted chain of organic parts, the plan of which existed in its seed and root. Man is similar to the tree. In the newborn child are hidden those faculties which are to unfold during life. The individual and separate organs of his being form themselves gradually into a harmonic whole."[22]

---

[22] F.V.N. Painter, *A History of Education* (New York: D. Appleton and Co. 1898), p. 1.

The various faculties or capacities which await development in the child are classed as physical, mental, and moral. To meet the ends of life, the body must grow, the mind must develop, and the moral nature must be trained. These powers, though at first existing in a germinal condition, contain within themselves large possibilities and a strong impulse toward development. The germinal powers start spontaneously into activity; the limbs become restlessly active; the senses open to objects of the external world; and cognition has its beginning. This growth or development, which gradually transforms childhood into youth, and youth into manhood, goes on according to definite laws, and may sadly be thwarted by neglect, or greatly promoted by judicious care.

During a considerable period of his early life man is helpless and ignorant; he is without the strength and knowledge necessary to maintain an independent existence. It is this fact that renders education a necessity. The process of physical and mental growth must be assisted and directed during the formative periods of childhood and youth. This is the function of education. Without its fostering care, no generation can be adequately fitted for the duties of life and the achievement of a worthy destiny.

The end of education is complete human development. This is attained by leading the several parts of man's nature to a harmonious realization of their highest possibilities. The finished result is a noble manhood. The elements of this manhood are a healthy body, a clear and well-informed intellect, sensibilities quickly susceptible to every right feeling, and a steady will whose volitions are determined by reason and an enlightened conscience.

While in its essential nature education aims at developing a noble type of manhood, it has also an external relation. Man has various labors and duties to perform in the world, which require special training and a wide range of knowledge. Childhood and youth are the periods of preparation. Hence, it is clear that education, both in its subjects and methods of instruction, should have some reference to the demands of practical life. Human development must therefore be combined with practical wisdom. This view is forcibly presented by Herbert Spencer. "How to live," he says, "that is the essential question for us. Not how to live in the mere material sense only, but in the widest sense. The general problem which comprehends every special problem is the right ruling of conduct in all directions under all circumstances. In what way to treat the body; in what way to treat the mind; in what way to bring up a family; in what way to behave as a citizen; in what way to utilize all those sources of happiness which Nature supplies; how to use our faculties to the greatest advantage of ourselves and others; how to live completely. And this being the great thing needful for us to learn, is, by consequence, the great thing which education has to teach. To prepare us for complete living is the function which education has to discharge; and the only rational mode of judging of any educational course is to judge in what degree it discharges such function."[23]

THE TWO ELEMENTS ENTERING INTO EDUCATION

There are two elements, logically distinguishable but practically inseparable, entering into education. These are development and the acquisition of knowledge. Without development, the individual lacks strength to grapple with the problems of life; and without knowledge, he remains a cipher in society. The great law underlying physical and mental development is self-activity. Every truly educated person is self-made. The various functions of the mind, whether perceiving, feeling, judging, or willing, must for a long period be called into frequent exercise in connection with objects, facts, relations, and truths, in order to become active, obedient, and strong.

---

[23] *Ibid.*, p. 4.

The basis of this activity is knowledge, which is as necessary for the development of the mind as food is for the growth of the body. While the mind, from the first, possesses all the germs of mental power, it is the appropriation of knowledge alone that converts its latent and apparently passive capacities into active capabilities. Education is not creative; it cannot give what Nature has withheld. It is limited by the pupil's individuality, which it can ennoble, but not radically change.

DIFFERENT FORMS OF EDUCATION

In some form or other, education is as old as the human race. Where the form of civilization has been low, education has been narrow and defective. Uncivilized communities do scarcely more than strengthen the body and cultivate the senses. Among no two nations of antiquity have the theory and practice of education been the same. It has varied with the different social, political, and religious conditions of the people and the physical characteristics of the country.

A cursory study of the history of education reveals that education was always defective, usually laying stress upon some peculiar phase of human culture to the neglect of others. Sometimes the physical was emphasized, sometimes the intellectual, sometimes the moral, sometimes the religious; but never all together in perfect symmetry.

THE LINKAGE BETWEEN DEMOCRACY AND EDUCATION

The very basis of a democratic society is an insistence on the importance of the development of the individual. The reason for this insistence is clear, for the better the individual the better will be the society of which he is a part, and the better the society, the more opportunity it will offer to its members for their individual growth and development.

Democracy's primary need is an educated citizenry. Education and democracy are bound up in an unending chain of cause and effect. More democracy means more widespread universal education, and more education of the right kind means more democracy.

THE DIFFERENCE BETWEEN EDUCATION AND INSTRUCTION

Education, as stated above, aims at "bringing out" an individual's natural gifts, developing the whole human being, helping him or her to become what he or she is potentially capable of becoming. "Instruction," on the other hand, "is the process of pumping information into the person." In his book *The Direction of Human Development*, Ashley Montague writes: "We must recognize that today, in the western world, we have too much instruction and all too little education. We are far too busy filling up the young with what we think they ought to know, to have much time left for helping them become what they ought to be."[24]

EDUCATION TODAY

The paramount aim of education today, it seems, is to prepare individuals for jobs, the marketplace, rather than for the art of living. The emphasis is on the acquisition of knowledge, skills, rather than the development of the total human being. The final product our system is turning out, in most instances, is one-sided, half-developed, maladjusted personalities. Little wonder so many people find themselves without direction, and without meaning for their existence. How can such individuals be expected to help shape the destiny of their

---

[24] Ashley Montague, *The Direction of Human Development* (rev. ed., New York: Hawthorne Books, 1970), p. 300.

form of government if they are helpless in shaping their own individual lives and destinies?

"We cannot take democracy for granted as something that is sure to endure.... We tend to think of it as something that has been established and that it remains for us simply to enjoy it."[25]

Democracy's future depends upon the health of its educational system; and its educational system's aim must not be less than helping all who are exposed to it realize their fullest potentialities. Anything short of that is bound to eventuate in democracy's erosion and decline.

---

[25] John Dewey, *The Problems of Men* (New York: Philosophical Library, 1946), p. 39.

14. Traits of Leadership

There are certain men whose lives make history, and long after they are gone their influence continues. Their personalities work upon us during their existence, and the memories of them excite our interest in the ideas and the ideals which they represented.

"We call our children and our lands," says Ralph Waldo Emerson, "by their names. Their names are wrought into the verbs of language, their works and effigies are in our houses, and every circumstance of the day recalls an anecdote of them.

"The search after the great man is the dream of youth and most serious occupation of manhood. We travel into foreign parts to find his works, if possible, to get a glimpse of him...."[26]

What is it that sets these figures apart from the rest of us? What traits must a person possess to be singled out as a leader?

WHY CERTAIN MEN RISE TO LEADERSHIP

There is no simple algebraic answer to our question. For any

---

[26] See Ralph Waldo Emerson's *Essay on Uses of Great Men*, First Edition. (New York: Wm. H. Wise and Co. Publishers, 1929).

attempt to describe the personality of a great man is an attempt at unraveling mystery. All we can hope to do is abstract from the typical leader a few of the traits which are generally attributed to him. Hence, if we ask what are the mental traits that distinguish a leader, our answer is that he must, in one way or another, be a great deal of a man or at least appear to be. He must stand for something to which men incline. It is impossible that he should stand forth as an archetype unless he is conceived as superior, in some respect, to all others within range of the imagination. He will always be found to owe his leadership to something strong, superior, affirmative, something that intrigues us.

To be a great man, a significant individual, means self-reliance. A person who does not cherish and trust a particular tendency of his own, different from that of other people and opposed by them in its inception, will not succeed in introducing anything of value. He has to be free from the influences and already defined purposes urged upon him by others, and come forth with something new. In other words, he must register his intense self. At the same time, his success in popularizing his special tendency depends upon his being in tune and in touch with the current of human life. In leadership, the matter of communication means the difference between failure and success. The able leader presents his ideas in such a congenial manner that they are seen by us as our own in a fresh guise.

DOES THE LEADER HAVE TO PROVE HIMSELF BY A DEED?

The opinion that leadership wholly depends upon a special deed, in which the power of the leader is manifested, is not necessarily true. For some unapparent reason we are often convinced of his power and the certainty of his success before his performance of the deed. There is something inexplicable about our immediate reaction to this causeless personal efficacy. It seems that his real greatness is self-evident and needs no particular works to substantiate it. "There are geniuses in trade, as well as in war, or the State, or letters; and the reason why this or that man is fortunate is not to be told. It lies in the man; that is all anybody can tell you about it. See him and you will know as easily why he succeeds as, if you see Napoleon, you would comprehend his fortune."[27]

In some strange way, the great personality injects us with the conviction that if he should be tried by a task he could perform it satisfactorily. There is a definiteness about him which indicates that in time of crisis he would not leave us drifting, that he would substitute action for doubt and set a course for us. By suggestion, he acts upon our minds, wins our approval, and makes us feel that in his hands, under his guidance and direction, we are safe.

At no time in his career does the genuine leader give us cause to doubt that our impressions of him are unreal, or that he is not completely wrapped up in the things he stands for.

> While thus he spake, his eye,
>   dwelling on mine,
> Drew me, with power upon me,
>   til I grew
> One with him, to believe as
>   he believed.[28]

Intellectually his ideas, his ideals, encompass what is best in our views, what is fit and timely. Emotionally, his beliefs draw our own into it. He knows how to dominate without awakening opposition.

In a sense, the great leader is also a conformist and follower. He leads by appealing to our own tendency and not by impos-

[27] See Ralph Waldo Emerson's *Essay on Character*, First Edition. (New York: Wm. H. Wise and Co. Publishers, 1929).

[28] Tennyson, *The Holy Grail*.

ing something external upon us. He is a symbol of the social conditions of his times under which he works.

Part of the mystery surrounding the leader is that there are others present in his day who are superior to him in many respects, but because of his traits or combination of them, he ascends, captures our attention, wins our faith, loyalty, and admiration.

THE MOST IMPORTANT ASPECT OF LEADERSHIP

The most important aspect of the leader is that he comes to us with an ideal around which he unites us, opens an outlet for our surplus energy, and sends us forward confidently towards the goal.

"It is true of races, as of individuals, that the more vitality and onwardness they have, the more they need ideals and a leadership that gives form to them. A strenuous people like the Anglo-Saxon must have something to look forward and up to, since without faith of some sort they must fall into dissipation or despair; they can never be content with the calm and symmetrical enjoyment of the present which is thought to have been characteristic of the ancient Greeks."[29]

The effect of the leader upon us is similar to that of the lover upon the object of his love. He makes us feel reborn. He brings new interest into our lives, into everyday happenings and into things to come. Our imagination is awakened, our thinking energized, our hopes lifted, our horizons extended.

Little wonder why such men change the course of events in their own time and leave an enduring influence upon future generations.

---

[29] Charles H. Cooley, *Human Nature and the Social Order* (New York: Charles Scribner's Sons, 1902, 1922), pp. 321-322.

15. The Value of Philosophy

PHILOSOPHY DEFINED

P hilosophy means "love of wisdom." It is the process and expression of rational reflection upon experience. Philosophy is the attempt to think clearly and methodically about certain concepts which are always turning up in our thinking and which seem necessary to our thinking, but which the special sciences do not tell us about. More fully, philosophy may be defined as the attempt to understand the universe, ourselves, and our place in the universe.

Questions to which definite answers have been found belong to the sciences. Questions to which there are no indisputable answers belong to the realm of philosophy. Philosophy concerns itself with such questions as these:

Has the universe any unity of plan or purpose, or is it a

fortuitous concourse of atoms? Is consciousness a permanent part of the universe, giving hope of indefinite growth in wisdom, or is it a transitory accident on a small planet on which life must ultimately become impossible? Are good and evil of importance to the universe or only to man?[30]

It cannot be maintained that philosophy can claim a great measure of success in its attempts to provide the answers to the questions it raises.

Philosophers seem to be in disagreement about everything under their scrutiny. They question everything and their answers are conflicting. A philosopher who is candid will admit that his study has not achieved any positive results such as have been achieved by the physical sciences.

Few men of practical affairs see any value in the study of philosophy. They regard it as a useless exercise of the mind; they view its study as nothing more than mental gymnastics without any benefits. The study of physical science, they argue, is useful, not only because of its effect upon the student, but also because of its benefits to all mankind. "But," they ask, "in what way does a knowledge of philosophy enhance our welfare?"

It must be admitted that philosophy will not improve our material welfare, add to our popularity, enhance our social status, or affect our lives directly.

Philosophy has no ascertained body of truth. It has not achieved any positive results in the past, nor does it expect to in the future. Any particular question to which there is a definite answer belongs to a body of knowledge other than philosophy. Only those questions to which there are no clear answers remain within the realm of philosophy. Of what value and importance then is philosophy?

---

[30] Bertrand Russell, *The Problems of Philosophy* (New York: Henry Holt and Company, Home University Library, No. 35), p. 241.

THE VALUE OF PHILOSOPHY

Philosophy, unlike the physical sciences, serves no utilitarian purpose. And yet, it has tremendous value, in that it reminds man of the utility of things which do not deal with means, but with ends. For man's life requires something more than mere material things. Man needs values and realities which transcend time. Man needs food for his spirit as he needs food for his body. He needs a reason for living, suffering, dreaming, hoping. Man's attitude toward life, his practical decisions depend on the answers he gives to those nagging, eternal, ultimate questions which philosophy asks.

"The man who has no acquaintance with philosophy," says C.E.M. Joad, "goes through life imprisoned in the prejudices, the preferences, the habitual beliefs derived from the society in which he happens to have been born and the period in which he lives."[31] Philosophy has the power of unchaining man from the prejudices, beliefs, customs, convictions, and principles which he inherited from his environment, and ideas which he carries in his mind, to which he never consented and which he never examined as to their worth. Through a study of philosophy, man's mind is liberated. He begins to see that the world extends beyond his family, his friends, his city, and his nation. He becomes more critical of his own thoughts and acts as well as those of others. He becomes more of a human being. Instead of finding himself living in a walled city, he discovers that he is a citizen of the infinite universe; and in contemplating infinity, his mind achieves some share in it.

But do we not live in a world and in a period of practicality in which facts are what really count? Is it not more advantageous to depend upon the sciences, which offer us exact data which we can put to use and to our immediate material advantage? Anything that is beyond utility has no place in our society, runs

---

[31] C.E.M. Joad, "Essay on Philosophy and Life" (New York: *Classics in Philosophy and Ethics*, Philosophical Library, 1960), p. 8.

the argument. If it were true that philosophy is completely divorced from science, that it has no interest in the facts accumulated by science, it could not function. However, there is a distinction between philosophy and science.

PHILOSOPHY AS DISTINGUISHED FROM THE SCIENCES

In distinguishing philosophy from the sciences, it may not be amiss to guard against the possible misunderstanding that philosophy is concerned with a subject matter different from, and in some obscure way transcending, the subject matter of science. By what, then, does philosophy distinguish itself from the sciences? By what does it distinguish itself, for example, from the science of astronomy, or from that of physics, biology, or of psychology? Not, certainly, by the difference of its matter. Its matter is quite the same as that of the various empirical sciences. Plan and order of the universe, structure and function of the human body, human behavior, etc., all belong to philosophy quite as much as to their respective special sciences. But if this is so, it may be asked what function can remain for philosophy when every portion of the field is already taken up by specialists? Philosophy claims to be the science of the whole; but if we get the knowledge of the parts from the different sciences, what is there left for philosophy to tell us? To this it is sufficient to answer generally that the synthesis of the parts is something more than that detailed knowledge of the parts in separation which is gained by the man of science. It is with the ultimate synthesis that philosophy concerns itself; it has to show that the subject matter which we are dealing with in detail really is a whole consisting of articulated members. The relationship between the sciences and philosophy is of reciprocal influence. The sciences may be said to furnish philosophy with its matter, but philosophical criticism reacts upon the matter thus furnished, and transforms it.

Such transformation is inevitable, for the parts only can exist and can only be fully and truly known in their relation to the whole.

THE PHILOSOPHER'S TASK

The task of the philosopher is to coordinate all the departments of knowledge. For the philosopher is essentially the man who, in Plato's description of him, takes a "synoptic" or comprehensive view of the universe as a whole.

"Psychology, sociology, and anthropology afford us invaluable and ever-growing material dealing with the behavior of individual and collective man and with the basic components of human life and civilization. This is an immense help in our effort to penetrate the world of man. But all this material, this immense treasure of facts, would be of no avail if it were not interpreted as to enlighten us on what man is. And it is up to the philosopher to undertake the task of interpretation."[32]

Philosophy is not satisfied with the mere coordination of the data produced by the various sciences; it inquires into their meaning. After combining the experiences of the scientist, the artist, the poet, and the common man, it seeks to learn what the nature of the universe must be in which such experiences are possible. In short, the philosopher is interested not so much in the facts which are made available to him, as in their meaning, their significance. The work of the philosopher begins where the scientist leaves off.

WHY THE PHILOSOPHERS DISAGREE AMONGST THEMSELVES

While the facts are the same for all the philosophers, their assessment of the facts, or evaluation of them, is not always the

---

[32] Jacques Maritain, *Essays to Leo Baeck* (London: East and West Library, 1954), p. 101.

same. For, in giving meaning to a set of facts, the philosopher injects his temperament and character into the act of assessment. This is one of the common reasons for the disagreement among the philosophers on some of the basic questions of life's purpose, or man's place in the universe, or good and evil. However, the fact that no agreed answer has yet been discovered to the most fundamental questions, cannot but suggest to the honest thinker that all systems of philosophy hitherto constructed are in some degree false.

The philosopher, aware of the conjectural knowledge which he attains through his search and study, is, nevertheless, not discouraged. His search for truth, and not essentially its attainment, is what he considers his reward. The philosopher's dedication to and endless search for truth not only offers him personal satisfaction, but it also indirectly benefits society.

In sum, the value of philosophy lies not in the answers it gives to the questions it asks, but in the questions themselves that it raises. "Through the greatness of the universe which it contemplates, the mind itself achieves greatness. It escapes from the circle of petty aims and desires which for most of us constitute the prison of everyday life, and, forgetting the nervous little clod of wants and ailments which is the self, is elevated into communion with that which is greater than the self. On the practical side this greatness of the mind generates qualities of tolerance, justice, and understanding, in the growth of which lies the chief hope for the world today."[33]

---

[33] C.E.M. Joad, *Essay on Philosophy and Life*, p. 14.

16. Ethics—The Science of Conduct

INTRODUCTION

Morality comes into play when man begins to reflect on his acts. Man's moral life, while it implies an intellectual element, is in its beginnings, and for a long time, a matter of instinct, of tradition, and of authority. Man's early conceptions of good and evil, right and wrong, virtue and vice, which guided his life, were largely accepted without questioning. The more man advanced intellectually, the more he began to rely on his own intelligence rather than on the commands of authority, tradition, and instinct. Eventually he developed an independent theory of life.

At what point in history morality passes from the instinctive to the reflective stage, either in the life of the individual or the race as a whole, remains conjectural. Even though an adequate moral theory was late in coming, still, it needs to be considered that practice to a large degree implies theory. Every life represents some conception of life's meaning. No life, as primitive as it may be, is completely haphazard.

Only the animal lives from moment to moment. As for man, each of his acts implies a purpose, a thought of something to be done, something worth doing. Each of man's acts does not stand alone; it is related to other acts, and these too are connected with still others—of the past, of the present, as well as of the future. The individual act of a human being is never an independent whole. It is a part of a totality. A person does not make up his mind afresh about each particular act. He refers to its place in the general scheme or plan of life by which he is governed, a plan which he has adopted at some point in the past. This plan or scheme of life may be regarded as a theory of life. Thus it is difficult to make an absolute distinction between the primitive, unorganized moral life and the more sophisticated type, which we think of as moral science. Ethical science is only a deeper, more systematic outlook on life, a more coherent reflection of it.

ETHICS DEFINED

Ethics is the science of conduct. It is a systematic inquiry into man's moral behavior the purpose of which is discovering the rules that ought to govern human action and the goods that are worth pursuing in human life. Can ethics be truly regarded as a science? Calling ethics a science means that its study represents an intellectual enterprise, a rational inquiry into its subject matter in the hope of gaining knowledge. Ethics shares with the empirical sciences a general methodology.

IS ETHICS A SCIENCE?

The attempt of all science is to rationalize our judgments, systematize them, and then explain them scientifically. Our judgments may be categorized as those of Facts and those of Worth—judgments of Is and judgments of what Ought to Be. The two different types of judgments represent two different types of science. One type of science seeks to organize into a rational system our Is judgments. The other type seeks to organize into a rational system our Ought judgments. The science dealing with judgments of Worth is called normative or appreciative.

The task of the natural sciences is to discover by reason the actual or phenomenal order—the order that characterizes "matters of fact." The aim of the normative or appreciative sciences is to discover, by reason, the ideal order which transcends the actual order. The natural sciences seek to discover the law or principle by which the facts of the universe can be described. The normative sciences seek to find the universal standard which would enable us to appreciate completely and consistently the facts of the universe. The natural sciences are involved in processes. The normative sciences have to do with products and their quality.

The function of the natural sciences is measurement; the function of the normative sciences is evaluation. The former finds rational order in the facts of the world and human life. The latter judges the facts of the world and life by reference to a rational order which transcends the facts themselves.

Ethics, like logic and aesthetics, is a normative or appreciative science—a science of value. The three sciences—ethics, logic and aesthetics—deal with our Critical judgments as distinguished from Factual judgments; they attempt to systematize these judgments by deducing them from a common standard of value. As it is the purpose of logic and aesthetics to interpret and explain our judgments of intellectual and of aesthetic value, so it is the purpose of ethics to interpret and explain our judgments of moral value.

ETHICS THE SCIENCE OF THE GOOD

In sum, as distinguished from the natural sciences, the sciences of the actual, ethics is the science of the Good. It is a normative science or a science of the ideal. It concerns itself not with what Is, but with what Ought to Be. What, it asks, is the ultimate Good in human life? To what common denominator can the various so-called "goods" of life be reduced? Why, in the last analysis, is life judged to be worth living? The task of ethics is the interpretation and explanation of our judgments of aesthetic and of logical or intellectual value. This task ethics seeks to accomplish by investigating the ultimate criterion or common measure of moral value, the true norm or standard of ethical appreciation.

Ethics, as the science of the Good, is the science of the ideal and the Ought.

17. Custom and Reflective Morality

MAN IS BORN A MORAL BEING

From the beginning of his existence man is found to be a moral being. If it were not so, he could never become moral, anymore than he could make any intellectual attainments if he were not from the start of his career an intellectual being.

THE TERM MORAL

The term "moral" is derived from the Latin word *mores*; it refers to customs which any given society considers essential to its welfare, and which it therefore enforces upon its members through the imposition of general pressures.

PRIMITIVE MORALITY

No human society—even the most primitive kind—could

exist without customs to which all its members are bound to conform and habitually do conform. Because many of these customs are essential to the preservation and perpetuation of the tribe or the community, the violation of them excites the resentment of the whole group. The primitive concept of "wrong" consists of an act by any of its members which evokes resentment of the whole group, and the idea of "right" consists of a deed which arouses the approbation of the whole community.

Conformity to standards of right and wrong is expected of every member of the group. Before a young man is admitted to the manhood of the tribe, certain tribal *mores* are impressed upon him. It is reported, for example, that among the Basutos a severe flogging is resorted to in order to fix the tribal injunctions of the group upon the young man's memory.

A few of the injunctions that the newly admitted member of the tribe is expected to remember are: "Do not steal; do not commit adultery; honor your parents; obey your chiefs."[34] Some Australian tribes initiate the new member with these injunctions: "Be obedient to your elders; share everything with your friends; live in peace; do not assault girls or married women."[35]

Thus, when we make a study of most primitive forms of human practices, we find features which characterize man's consciousness of moral obligation. Certain types of activity are approved and others condemned. Authority resides in custom, established usage, public opinion. To this authority the individual is responsible. From the first, man is a social being; the family or the tribe is the unit, and the individual has no interests apart from the tribal and domestic interests in which he shares.

Primitive man could not imagine himself apart from this

[34] George Foot Moore, *The Birth and Growth of Religion* (New York: Charles Scribner's Sons, 1934), p. 66.

[35] *Ibid.*, p. 66.

social relation, which prescribes to him the law of his conduct and punishes him for the violation of this law.

The social relation, whether tribal or domestic, is always in its essence a moral relation, and the consciousness of these relations and of their claim upon the individual life is the consciousness of moral obligation.

MAN'S MORAL PROGRESS

The fundamental law of moral progress may be said to be the gradual discovery of the individual, or even more precisely the individual's self-discovery. Individual moral independence and responsibility are the products of many centuries of moral development. In the early history of man, the ethical unit is the family or the tribe; later it is the State; still later it is the class; and, last of all, the individual. Aeons pass before we witness from the family and tribe, from the State and class, the emergence of the individual as an independent moral being. Even after the individual has differentiated himself from the larger social whole, much time passes before he gains a true understanding of himself and of his relation to society.

Not until the rise of industry does the individual gain a new importance and new rights. It is from this juncture onward that we notice moral progress. Aristocracy is superseded by democracy. The individual finds his place in the body politic and political disabilities are gradually removed.

As the individual emerges, he discovers not only himself but a life with his fellow citizens; he discovers a relation to all other human beings. He becomes conscious of the world, of humanity. His morality is no longer limited to his own group and reflective of a particular community. The law which guides his conduct is no longer outer but inner.

First, then, it is the outer law—the law of custom, accompanied by coercion in one form or another—that the individual obeys. This stage is one of passive, uncritical acquiescence.

As the individual advances to moral manhood, he passes from his allegiance to the outer law to the more stringent command which he finds written in his own heart. This stage may be described as the reign of the inner law of individual conscience, of the assertion of the right of private judgment in the moral sphere.

THE DIFFERENCE BETWEEN CUSTOM AND REFLECTIVE MORALITY

There is a marked difference between morality which flows from custom and independent, reflective morality. The standard of the good set up by custom morality is corporate rather than personal. Whatever custom morality approves and disapproves at no time reflects personal choice. Acceptance of the good or rejection of what is considered evil by custom morality is an acceptance or a rejection by pleasure, by pain, by habit, and not by choice. Custom morality preserves a fixed order. Its concern is the preservation of this order rather than the promotion of progress.

Custom morality is one of praise and blame based on the code which happens to be honored at a particular time in a particular social group. Whoever conforms to current practices receives praise, whoever deviates from the accepted norm of behavior exposes himself to censure and blame.

Reflective morality, instead of resorting to praise and blame for conformity and nonconformity, scrutinizes conduct objectively—that is, with reference to its causes and results. The concern of reflective morality is that a person shall discover for himself what he is doing and why he is doing it; that he shall be sensitive to consequences in fact and in anticipation, and shall be able to analyze the influences and forces which make him act as he does. In reflective morality approval and disapproval are subjected to judgment by a standard instead of being taken as ultimate.

THE EMERGENCE OF REFLECTIVE MORALITY

Reflective morality substitutes a rational method for setting up standards and forming values in lieu of habitual acceptance. Reflective morality emerges when the positive belief of what is right and what is wrong according to custom is abandoned and man begins to evaluate right and wrong in the light of reason.

Reflective morality is achieved only when the individual chooses the good freely, strives towards its fulfillment, and seeks a progressive social development in which all the members of society shall share.

Even though in reflective morality the course of action rests solely upon the conscience of the individual, yet it is imperative, according to Aristotle, that the doer of a moral act be possessed with a certain "state of mind" while performing the act. He must know what he is doing and choose to do the act, and the choice must be the expression of a recognized, stable character. For the act of an imbecile has no moral quality.

18. One Moral Law

"Die happy," said the Greek poet Pindar. "Thou canst not climb the brazen heaven", Pindar hinted. But man has mastered the secrets of the gods. He can climb the brazen heaven. He soars above the earth faster and to greater heights than the eagle; he plunges into the depths of the sea where no fish can follow. He has in a degree conquered the earth, the sea, the air, and even space.

There seem to be no bounds to man's capacity. Intoxicated by the advances he has made in biology and medicine, he dreams of discoveries which may arrest the processes of decay in the living organism, prolong indefinitely the period of human life, and even perhaps deliver us from the doom of our mortality.

What he dreams of achieving in the years to come, and what he will indubitably achieve, will make his accomplishments to this day appear almost primitive. Numerous worlds await his discovery and conquest; untold mysteries stand ready to surrender to his intellectual might.

Science through research is constantly outdoing itself. The invention of today is superseded by an improved one tomorrow. Progress is continuous in the material world. Every new breakthrough spells victory for man over nature. Each step forward leads to further adventures of the mind into the unknown. The satisfaction of discovery is boundless; the promises of new findings are titillating. The scientific eye is therefore focused on the future.

Every scientific discovery, every invention, brings untold benefits to the individual, to the nation, and the world. Science, amply and tangibly, rewards man for his efforts. Thus man is actuated to reach out for new objectives, new dramatic and exciting goals.

WHY MAN PROGRESSED MATERIALLY

Why is it that materially man has been able to move so fast and so far, while spiritually or morally he seems to be in a rut? The answer is quite simple. In dealing with the physical world, man discovered that the only way to wrest from it its locked-up treasures is to master and respect Nature's Law—which is one, eternal, immutable, and unbreakable. The more man sought the benefits and blessings of the physical world, the more he learned that nature responds only to the call of the intellect and is deaf to the cry of the emotions. In learning this precious lesson, man became lord over nature, and the road to material progress was opened to him.

Since it was not a matter of opinion as to what Nature's Law demands, since nature would have it no other way than that it be viewed, studied, and dealt with objectively, the human race was united under this stern principle. Man in one part of the world and in one age is compelled to bow to nature's demand in another part and in another age.

Nature's Law impressed upon the members of the human family that their inner differences, their individual feelings about God, life, death, immortality, manner of worship, and the like, have no bearing on its responses. Recognizing this inexorable truth, members of the human family were led to the acceptance of a common language of communication (mathematics), the agreement upon tasks to be done together, and the joining of hands and hearts in the performance of them.

WHY MAN FAILED SPIRITUALLY

Unfortunately, in the spiritual world man failed to discover One Law for his guidance and welfare. He viewed the spiritual world, not through his intellect as he did the physical world, but subjectively through his emotions. Thus he proclaimed various laws on which not all could agree as to which was the best and deserved complete allegiance. The spiritual realm then became an arena of many different, conflicting opinions; it divided the human race; it generated hate and often occasioned violence among the children of men.

In lieu of everyone marching together toward a common goal, toward a life of peace and brotherliness, individual nations and races choose their separate goals and pursue these in their separate ways. This has been the case from the time man appeared on the earth.

A GLIMMER OF HOPE

Today, there is a glimmer of hope and promise that the human condition as it prevailed in ages past might eventually improve. The wide chasm between man's material success and his spiritual failure is beginning to haunt him. He is beginning to sense that, as there is One Law governing the "outer world," so there must also be One Law for the "inner world." Differences separating man are now being examined for their validity and where found wanting, are eliminated. The likenesses among men are now being promulgated and emphasized. An effort is on the way to find a common denominator for all races and all creeds, all human kind. The fruits of this undertaking will be slow in ripening, but the expectation of the result is heartening and inspiring in itself. An objective approach as to how man can best live harmoniously with his brother man is slowly beginning to replace his subjective feeling about it. Man is beginning to regard his fellow man as a human being with the same desires and same agonies, seeking the same happiness, satisfaction, and self-realization. He is beginning to see that error of thought is the cause of separatism and that truth, once found, is the cause of unity and cooperation. He knows that aeons will elapse before the chasm between his material success and spiritual failure is breached. But he is awakening to the fact that it needs to be done and that he can cause it to happen.

IS ONE MORAL LAW CONCEIVABLE?

Is it conceivable that men conditioned by diverse religions, loyalties, and beliefs will agree someday on One Supreme Moral Law as their authority? More and more thinking individuals are of the opinion that this is possible. After all, they argue, do not the great figures of Moses, Jesus, Mohammed, and Buddha, together with a host of other spiritual figures, teach in essence the same thing? Do they not all hold up the ideal of love before all mankind as the Law of Life?

It needs to be remembered that until men came to realize that Nature's Law is One for all, much skepticism, disagreement, disappointment, and frustration had to be overcome. The same story will surely repeat itself in man's struggle to find One True Moral Law, a light and guide for all. In the end, he will find it—even as some of the more enlightened people have found it in the past, and as the more intelligent are aware of it now.

19. Freedom as Opportunity

Every human being is born free. Freedom and existence are indistinguishable. One does not first exist and then attain freedom. To be human is to be free. Life is an onward movement; it is change, growth, becoming. "Life," says Erich Fromm, "has an inherent tendency to expand, to express potentialities."[36] "Man," maintains Abraham Maslow, "has within him a pressure...toward unity of personality and identity...toward being creative...and he demonstrates this pressure toward fuller and fuller Being...in exactly the same naturalistic, scientific sense that an acorn may be said to be pressing toward being an oak tree."[37]

---

[36] Erich Fromm, *Escape from Freedom* (New York: Rinehart, 1941), p. 269.

[37] Abraham Maslow, *Toward a Psychology of Being*, 2nd Ed. (New York: Van Nostrand Reinhold Co., 1968), p. 153.

It may be said of each newborn child that he or she is a musical composer, artist, writer, poet, philosopher, statesman, sportsman, craftsman in the making. By virtue of his or her inner drive toward evolvement, each infant represents promise and hope for the future of mankind. As the Psalmist has it, "Out of the mouths of babes and sucklings hast Thou founded strength."[38]

Whatever man points to with pride as his great undying achievements on earth were at one time mere ideas, ideals, dreams, visions, locked up in his embryonic mind waiting for ripening, emergence, and ultimate concretization. What, after all, is civilization but the cumulative expression of human thought, desire, will, and action? Is it not the externalization of the inner man? Is it not a demonstration of man advancing, progressing from a lower to a higher level of consciousness, from a simpler to a more complex state of being, obeying nature's law of responding to his "inherent tendency to expand, to express potentialities"?

But if it is true that man is born free, how can we explain this age-old struggle for freedom? The answer to the question is embodied in our understanding of what is meant by the term freedom. Freedom is a complex concept varying in meaning from age to age, and from person to person living in the same society. Freedom to the enlightened and the benighted cannot and does not mean the same thing. Freedom is an elusive concept. If we are to do justice to the idea, it is imperative that we abandon the notion that it is something definite and final, something that can be grasped and held for all time. Freedom is an ultimate goal and as such can never be fully attained.

The best definition of freedom is perhaps nothing other than the most helpful way of thinking about it; and it seems that the most helpful way of thinking about it is to regard it in the light of the contrast between what a man is and what he might be.

---

[38] Ps. 8:3.

Even though man is free at birth, yet by himself he cannot fully develop. For the realization of his potentialities, he requires outside help. This help can be given only by the social order.

Too often we err in thinking that the individual is separate and apart from the social order, that society is a hindrance to man's natural development, that it imposes too many restrictions on his actions. The fact is that man has no existence apart from society and can realize himself only through it. A separate individual is an abstraction unknown to experience, and so likewise is society when regarded as something apart from individuals. The reason why most people think so naturally and easily of the individual phase of life is because it is a tangible one, the phase under which men appear to the senses, while the actuality of the group or nation or mankind at large is realized only by the active imagination.

Freedom is not, as it is commonly believed, the absence of social constraint, but rather an opportunity for right development. A child, for example, if cast away on a desert island, would, assuming that he succeeded in living at all, never know speech, or social sentiment, or any complex thought. On the other hand, if all his surroundings are from the first such as to favor the enlargement and enrichment of his life, he may attain the fullest development possible to him.

Now, how effectively a given society can serve as a means for growth and development of its members depends in no small measure upon its own level of development. To the degree that it is developed, to that same degree can it help its members in their unfoldment.

The social order is antithetical to freedom only insofar as it is a bad one. The fewer the opportunities it offers to its members for the realization of their potentialities—that is, schools, libraries, museums, newspapers, facilities for travel, choice of careers, and the like—the greater is the constraint on its citizens and the more limited is their freedom. On the other hand, in that society where the means and the opportunities for one's self-actualization are varied and numerous, there an individual will flourish, and with him also the society of which he is a member. In such a society, it may be said freedom reigns.

The struggle for freedom breaks out when and where people become aware that their "inherent tendency to expand" as full human beings is thwarted by the lack of these vital opportunities that are necessary for their evolvement.

Freedom as opportunity is best exemplified in the United States. In comparison with other lands, there is more opportunity here for a person to become in fact what he is in potentiality than anywhere else on the globe. Nevertheless, since man grows through opportunity, he will always seek more and more of it for his enlargement. So, even in a country where the social order offers more means to an individual for his self-realization than in any other, the Voice for Freedom is continuously sounded.

Man's struggle for freedom, it appears, shall never cease. "Let Freedom Ring" shall forever remain his motto.

20. Three Forms of Slavery and Three Types of Freedom

Negatives and positives are inseparable in the mind. Whenever we think of one, the other is consciously or unconsciously conjured up—like day and night, hot and cold, good and bad, sickness and health, slavery and freedom, etc.

In thinking of the latter two subjects, three distinct forms of slavery and three particular types of freedom come to mind.

The first form of man's enslavement occurs when he is still in his primitive state. At this point in time, he is dominated by nature. Nature appears to him to be his bitterest enemy, determined to destroy him. He is terrified by her in numerous ways, and by myriad means he attempts to pacify, befriend, and win her favor. Once he gains an understanding of her character, learns how to use her, he achieves what may be considered as the first type of freedom, which is Freedom from Nature.

The second form of enslavement is that of man's subjugation by his fellow man. As soon as man discontinues his nomadic life, roots himself in one place, then there arise in his midst self-proclaimed rulers who deprive him of his basic rights—his freedom. At first man does not fully realize that he has been disadvantaged. He imagines that his condition has been decreed by his gods. He therefore accepts his lot without complaint. But when in the course of time he reaches a higher level of intelligence, he becomes conscious that his freedom has been encroached upon. When this happens, dissent follows, rebellion sets in, a struggle ensues between the ruled and ruler.

In some instances man has succeeded in wresting from the enslaver the freedom that is rightfully his—such as in the democratic countries. In other instances such as in the dictatorial countries, the battle is still being fought in one way or another. In areas of the world where man triumphed over his oppressor, he is enjoying the second type of freedom—Freedom from Man.

The third form of enslavement is that which man experiences from himself. This form of servitude is not easily discernible. When man's freedom is thwarted by a force from the outside, sooner or later he becomes aware of it. But rarely would it occur to anyone that he might be his own enslaver.

In his essay *Master, Slave, and Freeman*, the noted philosopher Nicolas Berdyaev writes: "Man is a tyrant over himself by every sort of fear that is possible. He tyrannizes over himself by envy, by self-love...by the consciousness of his weakness and the thirst for power and greatness. By his enslaving will man enslaves not only another but himself."[39]

Those individuals who critically examine their lives, resolve to rid themselves of what Francis Bacon calls "Idols of the mind," such as false beliefs, prejudices, hatred, scapegoatism, and accept full responsibility for their omissions as well as commissions, acquire the truest type of freedom which is Freedom from Oneself.

---

[39] See "Master, Slave, and Freeman" by Nicolas Berdyaev, in *Four Existentialist Theologians* (New York: Doubleday & Co., 1958), p. 133.

21. Man in Pursuit of His Natural Rights

MAN'S INALIENABLE RIGHTS

From the earliest beginning of man's history till approximately the time of the eighteenth century, no loud outcry was heard concerning man's natural rights. However, from the eighteenth century and onward the idea that man possesses inalienable rights has been stressed in various declarations and pronouncements. In the United States Declaration of Independence it is held to be "self-evident, that all men are created equal, that they are endowed by their creator with certain inalienable Rights, that among these are Life, Liberty, and the pursuit of Happiness." The Virginia Bill of Rights affirms "that all men are by nature equally free and independent, and have certain inherent rights of which, when they enter into a state of society, they cannot by any compact deprive or divest their posterity; namely, the enjoyment of life and liberty, with the means of acquiring and possessing property, and pursuing and obtaining happiness and safety." In the Declaration of the Rights of Man and of Citizen, issued by the National Assembly of France in 1789 and prefixed to the French Constitution of September 1791, the "natural and imprescriptible rights of man" are listed as "liberty, property, security, and resistance of oppression."

Why is it that we hear so little about these natural rights prior to the eighteenth century? And if it is true that man possesses certain inborn rights, why was it necessary to declare them at all? And to whom were these declarations directed?

It was not until man became disenchanted with the powers that governed him, discontinued his trust and reliance on them, that he asserted in different documents and declarations the rights that are his as a person, and informed in one way or another the authority which he discredited that he is free of its rule.

HUMAN RIGHTS IN PRIMITIVE SOCIETY

Now let us trace the conditions and circumstances under which man lives from early times leading up to the point when he begins to assert his individuality and claim those rights which he believes belong to him as a person.

During the primitive period of his existence, man's authority are the customs, the *mores*, the approved ways of his tribe. The welfare of the group is regarded as in some sense imbedded in the customs which it follows. If anyone should decide to act contrary to them, he is made to feel the group's disapproval.

In the early forms of society there is no stage at which individual thought and action are free from the pressure of the social environment. The mind and will of individuals are dominated by the collective mind as expressed in the customs of the group.

HUMAN RIGHTS IN ANCIENT HEBREW SOCIETY

When the Hebrews entered the land of Canaan, Palestine, they brought with them their tribal customs, tribal morality. This group morality persisted until the advent of the eighth century prophets. It was they who effected a transition from group to individual responsibility.

Before the transition, all the kin was treated as guilty for the offense of the kinsman. In like manner, the family of the righteous man shared in the divine favor. The eighth century prophets pronounced a radical change. The saying, "The fathers have eaten sour grapes and the children's teeth are set on edge," is not to be used any more, declared Ezekiel, speaking for Yahveh. "The soul that sinneth it shall die; the son shall not bear the iniquity of the father, neither shall the father bear the iniquity of the son."[40]

Through the work of the prophets, the shift away from the group morality to individual responsibility began. The Hebrews, through the notion of individual responsibility as taught by the prophets, laid the foundation for what at a later period in world history was broadened into the concept of individual rights.

HUMAN RIGHTS IN GREEK SOCIETY

In vain we look for the idea of individual rights in the classical exponents of Greek ethics. In his dialogues, Plato's treatment of justice as a general feature of the good life rather than a particular phase of it obscures its application to the question of rights. What emerges is that the aim of civic society is to do the fullest justice to the capacities of individuals by assigning each his place in an organized system of social purposes.

---

[40] Ezekiel, 18:20.

Plato, in his *Republic*, is so confident in the ethical supremacy of the State, so convinced of the absoluteness of its value, that he would make it the sole criterion of individual virtue. Plato does not conceive any distinction or antagonism between the good of the individual and that of the State. He does not differentiate between the citizen and the man. Those who cannot discharge the duties of citizenship, according to Plato, the helplessly weak and incurably sick, ought not to be allowed to live. In Plato's ethic there is no concept of personal rights as understood by those living under Western democracy today.

In Aristotle we see the beginning of a change from the State to the individual. In his view the individual is an end in himself, and the State but the medium of his ethical life. Still, Aristotle, like Plato, maintains that man apart from the State would not be a moral being. Thus, while Aristotle starts out in the direction of the individual and his rights as a human being, he never gets to that point.

HUMAN RIGHTS IN ROMAN SOCIETY

In early Roman law, which did so much to develop the idea of personality, the idea of duty is far more prominent than that of rights.

Duty in Roman society was, indeed, the inner correlate of a social and political system that made law and government supreme. Cicero held that, as a rational being, man ought to recognize the law of reason. As a human being, he is endowed by nature with a sense of order, decency, and propriety. He should therefore conform to the law of nature and respond to the intrinsic worth of what is honorable. And, as a member of society, a status which is deeply rooted in nature, man ought not injure his fellow or do anything to disrupt the social bond. In short, duty, the Romans stressed, is man's response to the law of his being.

HUMAN RIGHTS UNDER CHRISTIANITY

In its very early beginning Christianity taught the supreme value of the individual as a moral being. It recognized no distinction between the rich and the poor, the cultured and the uncultured, the freeman and the slave. The Christian ideal was from the first emphatically a social as well as an individual ideal; it was a gospel for human society as well as for the individual man. Gradually however, the ecclesiastical polity came to resemble the civil, and the *Civitas Dei* became also an earthly State.

The individual was subordinated to the ecclesiastical State. This meant the subordination of morality, of ethics, to politics. The Church became the keeper of the individual conscience. The concern of the Church was not the secular part of conduct, not the moral phase of life, but its sacred and religious part—the performance of certain ceremonies, the doing of certain outward acts, rather than the inward conformity of the spirit to the rule of Christianity. Instead of deepening and quickening the conscience of the individual, the Church deadened it.

HUMAN RIGHTS DURING THE PERIOD OF THE RENAISSANCE AND REFORMATION

The periods of the Renaissance and Reformation saw the rise of nationalism and of civil and religious liberty. The formation of national states tended to strengthen the sovereignty of such governments in opposition to the unity of Europe for which Church and pope had stood. It was a breaking away from the rule of Rome. The act of Henry VIII in proclaiming himself Head of the English Church was a dramatic expression. It tended to substitute patriotism for religion as supreme authority. At the same time a middle class of merchants, craftsmen, and yeomen emerged which led in the struggle for civil and political liberty. During the eighteenth century the doctrine of natural rights became a symbol of the growing strength of the individual, asserting itself as over against the formerly claimed divine right of monarchs.

HUMAN RIGHTS DURING THE PERIOD OF ENLIGHTENMENT

The period of Enlightenment witnessed a general change of the widest range and deepest significance in the temper and attitude of the peoples of Northern and Western Europe. Tendencies which were at work in the Renaissance and Reformation periods became everywhere dominant in the eighteenth century. The world of thought and culture was transformed. The humility, the self-distrust, the dependence upon supernatural powers, the submission to external authority, the passive acceptance of existing conditions, the belief that amelioration can come only in another world beyond the grave, the renunciation of the world and its pleasures—all of which characterized the Middle Ages—were widely overcome, and men faced life with a new confidence in themselves, with a new recognition of human power and achievement, with a new appreciation of present values, and with a new conviction of the onward progress of the race in the future.

The vast number of discoveries of physical science and the advancing conquest of the forces of nature gave men a growing sense of mastery over their environment, and the promise of ever more secrets to be disclosed, ever new victories to be achieved, made the world far more fascinating than it had been. The idea of indefinite progress and the expectation of a continuous advance in human culture and the betterment of the conditions of early life kindled the enthusiasm of an ever-enlarging circle. Discontent with existing conditions of one sort and another increasingly took the form of agitation rather than resignation, until finally the man who tamely and piously submitted to industrial oppression or economic injustice, consoling himself with the picture of a future life where all would be well, became an object not of admiration, as in the past, but of contempt. The fruits of the spirit of the Enlightenment were seen in every sphere—religious, social, scientific, economic, political, philosophical, industrial, and ethical.

In the political sphere, the Enlightenment promoted constitutionalism, laid the foundations of democracy, undermined belief in the supernatural origin of the State and the divine right of kings. Institutionalism gave way to individualism in every line, and reverence for the great political, social, and religious institutions of the past rapidly waned.

Developing industry and commerce completed the destruction of feudalism and contributed to economic freedom and to the disappearance of time-honored social distinctions.

Culture was becoming largely secular. Intellectual leadership had passed from the clergy to the laity and education from the Church to the State. Morality was divorced from theology and acquired a value of its own.

In philosophy, rationalism took the place of the old theological method. Truth was to be known by its clearness and self-consistency, rather than by the testimony of tradition and revelation. The doctrine of future rewards and punishments, which constituted an essential precept of both revealed and natural religion, was considered out of place by individuals who no longer believed in the needs of outside supports for their virtuosity.

The application of reason to religion reached its zenith, and Christianity was subject to a scrutiny of the most minute and exhaustive character. What happened in this period was not that reason then began to be applied to Christianity, but that reason was differently interpreted. The intellectual atmosphere of the Enlightenment, the general spirit and attitude, was literally unlike that of the Middle Ages. For in the Middle Ages the application of reason to religion merely meant the confirmation, not the criticism, of old ideas and dated theology. In the period of Enlightenment, the application of reason to religion resulted in the criticism and repudiation of the old beliefs.

The great achievement of the period of Enlightenment in the intellectual development of the individual was that the human mind came to realize the part it was itself playing in the whole realm of science and conduct. Man began to look within. For of a sudden it was dawning upon him that, if he was then living upon a higher level of knowledge and conduct than the animal or savage, this must be due to the activity of the mind. This was no creation of instinct or habit; nor could it be explained in terms of sense, or feeling, or impulse alone; it was the work of the more active, universal, and creative type of intelligence which we call reason. Man, as capable of such achievements in science and conduct, must be regarded with new respect. As having political rights, freedom, and responsibility, man has the dignity of a citizen, sovereign as well as subject. As guiding and controlling his own life and that of others by the power of ideas, not of force, he has the dignity of a moral person, a moral sovereignty. The controlling principle of the New Age was the worth and ability of man, a controlling ideal his independence and self-reliance.

HUMAN RIGHTS AS A RESULT OF THE AMERICAN AND FRENCH REVOLUTIONS

The American and French Revolutions marked a crisis in government. Both emphasized democracy, not only in its aspect of liberty and self-government, but in the meaning of equality. They contributed powerfully to leveling the distinctions fixed by birth between classes. The American nation was, in Lincoln's words, "conceived in liberty and dedicated to the proposition that all men are created equal." The French made Liberty, Equality, and Fraternity their creed.

The spread of self-government and equality has had a fundamental influence upon morals, as regards the general attitude toward authority. When people make their own laws they do not readily accept any moral standard or law which rests on authority of a ruling class, or of elders, or of church, or of school, unless it can justify itself by some other test.

Man did not become fully aware of his inalienable rights until the eighteenth century, the period of Enlightenment. It is only when man became enlightened that he first began to realize that his will played no role in the governing of his life; that he was being manipulated in various forms, and that as long as he accepted this manipulation as if it were the expression of his own will, he had no reason to rebel and protest against the operating forces and powers.

22. The Voice of Conscience

F or a harmonious, satisfying life, man needs to achieve a happy and healthy relationship with his fellow man. And basic to such an achievement is sensing the difference between right and wrong in all his thoughts and acts.

It is not always easy to know right from wrong. In many instances what is considered right or good in one place and at one time is regarded as wrong or evil in another place at another time. Even in the same place and at the same time what some consider right, others consider wrong. What aid can one enlist that would guide him in his decisions and acts?

Long ago gifted men asserted that there is no outward, infallible moral authority to direct human conduct. "Let a man obey his conscience, his inner voice, and he will not err." What is meant by conscience?

THE TERM CONSCIENCE

The term "conscience" is derived from the Latin *conscientia*, which meant originally "joint knowledge" or the knowledge which we share with others. It soon came to denote, however, consciousness or self-consciousness. It was not until modern times that the terms "conscience" and "consciousness" were differentiated. Consciousness in our times is understood as a purely intellectual function, a generic term for the phenomena of mind, or for that concomitant of mind which is called by some as the "complement of the cognitive energies." Conscience, on the other hand, is a name for the function of distinguishing between right and wrong.

CONSCIENCE IS TWO-SIDED

Conscience is two-sided; it has an intellectual as well as an emotional side. It may be enlightened and sensitive or the reverse. Its enlightenment hinges on the moral ideal of the individual; he may obey the moral law through fear of punishment here or hereafter, or simply to realize the ideal self. The man who is motivated to act on the basis of the highest ideal, who seeks to attain the best life of which humanity is capable, is governed by the most educated conscience.

TWO STANDARDS BY WHICH ACTS ARE JUDGED

There are two different standards by which men's consciences judge their acts. One standard is that of custom. The majority of men are governed by the moral opinion and attitude of their particular social set. Conscience in this instance is no more than one's consciousness of the disapproval of his friends at his daring to break ranks with them. In this situation conscience may be regarded more as social than moral. It is a low form of conscience serving to keep men as they are. It is timid of moral experiments; it is ever ready to persecute heretics and innovators and is apprehensive of new ideals, new patterns of behavior.

History is replete with examples of the lower type of conscience at work. It recalls the bitterness of the Roman citizen against those who condemned gladiatorial games. It reminds us of the animosity of the slaveholders against the apostles of freedom, the cruelties to which Galileo was exposed because he claimed the earth revolved around the sun, and the death sentence imposed upon Socrates for teaching what he believed to be truth. These few examples should bring to mind numerous others from our own day.

A second and higher standard to which conscience tends to grow is beyond the custom of the group, the nation, or the sect. It is at the same time individual and universal. Whatever others think or say or do, "this," says conscience, "is right for me." But it is made to be right for me because, profoundly, my act belongs to the universe as I belong to the universe; it is good for all men, for all time. This is the voice of the higher type of conscience.

The two types of conscience mentioned above, the lower and higher, are described by Erich Fromm as authoritarian and humanistic. According to Fromm, the authoritarian conscience, often mistaken for one's own "small voice," may be the voice of parents, teachers, religious leaders, the State, public opinion, all recognized authorities. These authorities are consciously or unconsciously accepted by people as ethical and moral legislators. Once the laws and sanctions of the authorities are adopted and internalized, then a person feels responsible to the external, internalized command, as if his own voice were speaking to him.

Humanistic conscience, according to Fromm, is not the internalized voice of authority which one obeys or is afraid to disobey, but rather one's own voice independent of external sanctions. One's own conscience is the reaction of one's own total personality. The humanistic conscience is a reaction of one's self to himself. It is one's own true voice beckoning him to himself. It is the voice which protects one's integrity.[41]

In many instances, both the lower and higher, the authoritarian and humanistic type of conscience, are present—not necessarily in separate individuals, but rather in the same person. There are times when a man will, with all his might, attempt to defend an outmoded ritual, practice, usage, or law, which he finds hard to forsake and which is also honored by his group. At another time, the same man will act in behalf of a universal cause at the sacrifice of friend and fortune. He will stand alone if necessary and so act as if he were representing all mankind. This is conscience expressed in its highest, noblest, purest form.

THE AUTHORITY OF CONSCIENCE

The notion once prevailed that, unless conscience had a Divine origin, its authority was impaired. In other words, its validity was made to depend on its creative origin instead of upon its judgment of facts. It is now generally held, as in all other scientific and philosophic problems, that the historic origin does not determine validity and that the authority of conscience depends on the same criteria as those which determine ordinary truths, and not upon any contingency of its source. We do not make any scientific truth depend on the cause of its origin, but upon its conformity to the facts and the law of things. It must be the same with the dictates of conscience.

---

[41] Erich Fromm, *Man for Himself* (New York: Holt, Rinehart and Winston, 1947), pp. 158-159.

23. The Functions of the State

ORIGIN OF THE STATE

Three different theories have been suggested for the origin of the State. The first traces government or the State to the Deity. Another aspect of this theory bases temporal sovereignty on a divine right. The second theory claims that government and sovereignty were founded by the consent of the people through an unwritten contract between them, and that the people in this contract reserved to themselves the right to rebel should the ruler abuse the authority they had entrusted to him. The third theory advances the belief that government or the State has been established on the basis of expediency and that this therefore accounts for the different existing stages of its development.

Neither the divine right theory not the contract theory offers a satisfactory explanation of the origin of government. It appcars that the most plausible theory is the one which founds government on expediency. (Plato, *Rep.* ii, 369)

THE STATE AS AN ETHICAL INSTITUTION

The State is an ethical institution, and as such it has two specific ethical functions: (1) that of creating for the individual the opportunity of self-realization, by protecting him from the encroachments of other individuals and non-political forms of society through the function of Justice; (2) that of improving the conditions of the ethical life of each of its citizens—through the function of Benevolence.

In executing its first ethical function of Justice, the State is called upon, above all else, to protect the individual in all the aspects of his life. From an ethical standpoint the State exists for the person and not the person for the State. The ethical function of the State is therefore to aid the person in the proper development of his personality. It is the medium of his moral life.

THE STATE AS THE PROTECTOR OF THE INDIVIDUAL

In order to protect the individual from the encroachments of other individuals and of society, the State is forced to be in some considerable measure "aggressive." The tyranny of the individual as well as unofficial public opinion are ofttimes incomparably worse than what some refer to as the tyranny of the State. The purpose of State interference in all its forms is aimed at protecting the interest of individual freedom.

THE STATE AS PROTECTOR OF PROPERTY RIGHTS

The State is not only the custodian of "personal" rights but also the real rights of the individual. Real rights or rights of property are essentially like all personal rights. The State therefore must not only establish the right of the individual to that which belongs to him, that which is his "own," but also the right of disposition of that which is his own. This does not mean, of course, that the individual is free to use his property or dispose of it in a manner that will cause hurt to his fellow. The individual cannot isolate himself in his conduct from other individuals. He must always remember that his life is interwoven with the lives of others. Hence, if his possessions are used by him unethically and become an instrument of moral evil to other citizens, it behooves the State to interfere. It is the duty of the State to guard a citizen's personal rights. Private ownership is thus limited by the State on the principle that the free and equal self-development of all its citizens is under its supervision of Justice.

THE STATE AS PROTECTOR OF SOCIAL INSTITUTIONS

As the State protects the individual from the encroachments of others, so too does it protect all those social institutions which depend upon it for their existence. Each of these minor societies has a sphere of its own which the State preserves from invasion by any of the others, and which the State itself must not interfere with. Each of these institutions has its own special function and its particular genius. It is the duty of the State not only to protect the existence and functions of these institutions, but also to make certain that the institution which it is guarding is maintained in its integrity and permitted to fulfill its own work and mission. In the performance of this duty the State may be called upon to improve the conditions of institutional life so that that life shall be helped to pursue its own course without interference or assistance from without.

All that is ethically imperative is that within these institutions freedom of initiative and self-development be allowed; that each institution be permitted to work out its own destiny, its own career, and realize its set purpose. At the same time, these social institutions must not be allowed to interfere with the functions of the State.

THE STATE AND ITS MAINTENANCE OF ORDER

Members of the State who violate the rights of others are punished. It is through punishment that the State can preserve the system of rights and obligations. From the viewpoint of the citizen, individual punishment means the forfeiture, temporary or permanent, of his rights as a citizen or of his civil liberty. This forfeiture is warranted only insofar as it is necessary in the interest of the common good which the individual had injured; since he has violated the conditions of social well-being, he is responsible for his own punishment as the new condition of that well-being, which includes his own. The social justice of punishment is evoked by its social necessity. The measure in which it exceeds that necessity is the measure of its injustice.

The object of punishment is not retribution in the sense of retaliation. The chief purpose of punishment is simply prevention or deterrence. Its justification is based on its effect on others rather than on the criminal. Its value is social rather than individual. The measure of the punishment is governed by the social necessity, and this measure is a changing one. A punishment which may be just and socially approved at an earlier stage in society, such as capital punishment for theft, becomes unjust because it is no longer socially approved at a later period. Generally it may be said that with social progress, with the development of the social spirit or the spirit of citizenship, the necessity of punishment gradually decreases. As man's will becomes more completely socialized, the role of force becomes less important.

THE STATE AND ITS FUNCTION OF BENEVOLENCE

The second of the ethical functions of the State is Benevolence. While there are social institutions within the State dedicated to the improvement of the lot of its citizens, there are areas where the action of the State because of its resources can be more efficient than any individual or any group. An example of only one of these areas is caring for the education of its citizens. The protection of the individual not only involves guarding his rights and liberties, it also implies, especially in a democracy, protecting him from the evils of ignorance. Compulsory, and under certain circumstances free education thus falls under the province of the State.

Besides concerning itself with the education of its citizens, it is the duty of the State in the interest of security to remove as far as possible the stimulus to crime which in most cases is the result of extreme ignorance and poverty. In this attempt it is necessary for the State to regulate the conditions of the industrial life in order to secure to each citizen the opportunity of earning an honest livelihood. By undertaking the burden of providing the citizen with the opportunity of self-maintenance, the State then is relieved of the greater burden of maintaining him.

Benevolence is a higher form of justice. It is for the State to improve the social conditions of the masses, to enable those who toil for the wealth of the nation to become sharers of it. To the "working classes" the State must give not merely the political franchise, but the ethical franchise for a full, worthy human life. As the custodian of the moral interests, and not merely the material interests, of its citizens, the State must see to it that the former are not sacrificed to the latter. While the industrial life is to be permitted to follow its own economic laws, as long as such independence is in keeping with ethical well-being, yet it is incumbent upon the State to coordinate the industrial with the ethical life. Industry is a human activity, and as such must be governed by the ethical as by the economic law. The State alone in this instance can enforce this regulation. This means, of course, State interference with the industrial life of Society;

but such interference is adjusted to the moral sense of the community.

If it is the function of the State to help its citizens to develop their highest manhood, then it becomes its duty to provide its citizens with a certain amount of leisure—particularly the working classes, which need it most. This again brings the State into the life of the industrial society, but the State as the all-inclusive social unity must guard and foster the ethical life of its citizens in the industrial as in the other spheres of that life.

Another duty of the State, assigned to it by its ethical constitution, deals with the distribution of material wealth. It is for the State to see to it that the struggle of the masses for mere physical existence does not consume all their energies, but that each individual in these masses has the opportunity for the realization of his higher ethical capacities. In this regard it is the State's responsibility to prevent the unequal distribution of its fortunes which might render the moral life of an individual impossible. In brief, it is for the State to so improve the conditions of human life, or the environment, that those who find themselves discriminated against, either by economic law or some other social impediment, will not be frustrated in their ethical goals and aspirations.

THE STATE AS REPRESENTATIVE OF THE WILL OF THE PEOPLE

The State's power of Punishment appeals to the citizen to exercise restraint on his activities, on his conduct. Although on the surface the action of the State seems to interfere with the freedom and will of the citizen, yet a close analysis will reveal that the will of the State is aimed at carrying out the will of the ethical person. The sovereign will represents the individual will or, more correctly, the general will of its citizens. For in the general will of the people, in the common personality of the citizens, is the true seat of sovereignty.

The supreme power in the State, whatever be the form of government, must be regarded as the "public person," and in obeying it the citizens are obeying their common personality. The sovereign power is "the public person vested with the power of the law, and so is to be considered as the image, phantom, or representative of the commonwealth...and thus he has no will, no power, but that of the law."[42]

Obedience to the State is obedience to the citizen's own better self. The individual may criticize the political order as an adequate version of the moral order. He may try to improve upon and reform it. However, where the State stays within the limits of its functions, he may not openly violate its order.

WHEN THE STATE MISREPRESENTS THE WILL OF THE PEOPLE

What if the State fails to reflect the will of the people? And what if the State should venture to step beyond its proper functions? What then should be the position of the citizens within it? Under such circumstances the citizens are duty bound to rebel. This action of the citizens should not be interpreted as an expression of disloyalty to the law and the constitution of the State. On the contrary, rebellion against the State, when it invades the rights of its citizens instead of protecting them, is to be regarded as a laudatory service to the nation.

As soon as the State ceases to represent the general will, so soon does it become necessary to replace the leadership of the State with representative leadership.

---

[42] John Locke, *Treatise of Civil Government*, bk. II, Chap. xiii.

24. Man's Chief Good

What, among the things life has to offer, may be considered as man's chief good?

Three different ethical theories which originated in the Greek world claim to have the answer to the question. One theory is referred to as Hedonism, the other Rationalism, and the third Eudaemonism.

MAN'S CHIEF GOOD ACCORDING TO HEDONISM

A study of man's nature led the Greek philosopher Aristippus of Cyrene (435-366 B.C.), founder of the Cyrenaic school, to conclude that man is fundamentally a sentient being; and if man is essentially a sentient being, his chief good can be no other than physical pleasure.

Aristippus disagreed with Socrates' observation that the true wisdom of life lies in foresight or insight into the significance of our actions, in accurate calculation of their results, pleasurable and painful, in the distant as well as in the immediate future, and also that the pleasures of the soul are far more preferable to those of the body. Aristippus maintained that the pleasure of the body is more intense than that of the soul, the pleasure of the moment more preferable to the doubtful pleasure of the future, and calculations of their results a futile exercise of the mind.

Man, according to the Cyrenaic philosopher, in order to realize his highest and only good in life, which is pleasure, must count each of his allotted moments and make the most of them. Sacrificing the present to the future, as Socrates would have us do, is folly in the eyes of Aristippus. Man, he stresses again and again, is a child of time, of the momentary present. If he wishes to realize that which he wants most, if he wishes to acquire life's chief good, he must surrender himself to the present joys of life, satisfying his physical desires.

Do not the reflections of Omar Khayyám echo the very assertions of Aristippus?

> Come, fill the Cup, and in the fire of Spring
> Your Winter-garment of Repentance fling:
>   The Bird of Time has but a little way
> To fly—and lo! the bird is on the wing.
> I must adjure the Balm of life, I must,
> Scared by some after-reckoning ta'en on trust,
>   Or lured with hope of some Diviner Drink,
> To fill the cup—when crumbled into Dust!
> Oh threats of Hell and hopes of Paradise!
> One thing at least is certain—this life flies;
>   One thing is certain, and the rest is Lies:
> The flower that once has blown forever dies.[43]

In the company of Omar's thoughts we also find those of the author of Ecclesiastes who wrote: "Too much wisdom is much

---

[43] *Rubaiyát of Omar Khayyám*. trans. Fitzgerald (London: 1859).

grief and he that increaseth knowledge increaseth sorrow....
For what hath man of all his labor, and all the vexation of his
heart, wherein he hath labored under the sun?... Then I commended mirth, because a man hath no better thing than to eat,
and to drink, and to be merry; for that shall abide with him of
his labor the days of his life which God giveth him under the
sun."[44]

Epicurus (341-270 B.C.), founder of the Epicurean school in
Athens, where the art of rational living was taught, like Aristippus contends that the end of life is pleasure, but that this end
is unattainable without the aid of reason. It is reason alone, he
holds, that makes possible the most perfect gratification of
feeling. It is through reason that pain is reduced to a minimum,
thus providing man with a deeper, intenser, more enduring
pleasure.

While it is true that pleasure is man's highest good, Epicurus
philosophizes, nevertheless he must call upon reason to help
him choose his pleasures discriminately.

"Since pleasure is our first and native good," says Epicurus,
"for that reason we do not choose every pleasure whatsoever,
but ofttimes pass over many pleasures when a greater annoy-
ance ensues from them. And ofttimes we consider pains superior to pleasure, and submit to the pains for a long time when it
is attended with a greater pleasure. All pleasure, therefore,
because of its kinship with our nature, is a good, but it is not in
all cases our choice even as every pain is an evil, though pain is
not always, and in every case, to be shunned. It is, however, by
measuring one against the other, and by looking at the conven-
iences and inconveniences, that all these things be judged.
Sometimes we treat the good as an evil and the evil, on the
contrary, as a good."[45]

---

[44] Ecc. 1:18, 1:3, 1:22-24.

[45] *Letter of Epicurus* (W. Wallace's Epicureanism London: 1880), pp.
129-31.

THE RATIONALISTS' IDEA OF MAN'S CHIEF GOOD

Plato and Aristotle are exponents of the Rationalists' view of life. Both taught that the life of virtue is a life according to right reason and that the vicious life is the irrational life. Both, however, distinguish two degrees of rationality. First, there is the guided life of sensibility. But beyond that, there is the higher life of reason itself.

The Rationalists hold that man's chief good is to be sought within, not without, in excellence of character and not in pleasure. The life of the wise man is the passionless life of reason. There is only one thing that belongs to the soul of man and that is reason. This is man's true inner good. The life of pleasure, the Rationalists contend, is a life of folly. The riches of the soul can be attained only by giving up the illusive, deceitful riches of pleasure. It is not an easy undertaking, they agree. It requires self-denial and strength of will. It means that a person is to reduce his desires to a minimum, that he is to live simply. The reward for such a life, they are convinced, can be peace of mind, something man craves more than wealth, more than pleasure. Anyone who achieves such a life, according to the Rationalists, has virtually conquered the worst of all his fears, death itself.

In brief, Rationalism predicates its philosophic expression of man's chief good on the idea that fundamentally reason, rather than sensibility, is the regulative principle in the life of a human being—that is, that his life must be one of pure reason if he is to realize his highest good.

MAN'S CHIEF GOOD ACCORDING TO
EUDAEMONISM

The Greek thinkers searched their hearts and minds to find what may be considered man's greatest good, his highest end in life. Thus, one school of thought maintained that pleasure is to be pursued. Another school suggested Rationalism as the road that leads to life's highest good. A third school came up with a philosophy called Eudaemonism (derived from the Greek word *Eudaimonia*, meaning happiness or well-being).

Eudaemonism, a theory of which Socrates was the strongest protagonist, rejects the hedonistic idea that man's chief good is self-gratification. It also disagrees with the Rationalists that man can achieve his highest good through self-sacrifice or self-denial. Instead, it advances the idea that man's greatest good lies in self-realization or self-fulfillment.

The Cyrenaics or Hedonists harped a great deal on the sentient self of man. The Rationalists concerned themselves largely with the rational self. In suggesting that man should strive for self-realization did the Eudaemonists have some special self in mind? The answer is yes. They were thinking of the total self.

According to Eudaemonism, the total self is what constitutes human personality and distinguishes man as a person from the animal or impersonal self. Man, say the Eudaemonists, is a self in the animal sense of selfhood. He is a creature of impulse, or subject to immediate wants and instincts which demand their satisfaction. The impulsive forces spring up in him as spontaneously as they do in the animal. These forces in the animal in their total workings constitute the animal's nature and goal. And if might were right, the same would be true of man. But for man, might is not right. Man is a rational being. Man as a rational being is called upon to bring impulse under the law of the rational self. The distinctive characteristic of man is that he has the power of reflecting upon his impulses and of viewing them in relation to a permanent total good.

In view of our definition of the total self, or personality, we may say that self-realization means that the desires in man, instead of being allowed each to pursue its own course and seek its own satisfaction, are so coordinated, correlated, and organized that each becomes instrumental in serving the rational self as a whole. This power of rising above the impulse of the moment, of transcending the sentient life, is what makes man, ethically, man.

Man has to constitute himself as a moral person. Out of feeling, impulse, and instinct, he is called upon to rise to the structure of ethical manhood. The same lesson, is presented by Matthew Arnold:

> Know, man hath all which Nature hath,
>   but more,
> And in that more lie all his hopes of
>   good.
> Man must begin, know this, where Nature
>   ends;
> Nature and man can never be fast friends.
> Fool, if thou canst not pass her, rest
>   her slave!

The good of a moral life, its ideal, is the achievement of a spontaneity, a freedom, and a naturalness like that of the life of original impulse. Virtue is to become second nature. When man reaches this state in his moral life, he enjoys the reward of self-fulfillment and self-realization.

Through the total-self, through his personality, through self-realization, man learns the difference between mere momentary pleasure and genuine happiness. He learns that pleasure is transitory and relative, enduring only while some special activity endures. Happiness is permanent and universal. It results only when the act is such a one as will satisfy all the interests of the self concerned, or will lead to no conflict either present or remote. Happiness is the feeling of the whole-self, as opposed to the feeling of some one aspect of self.

In sum, Eudaemonism claims that man's highest good is self-realization, through which means he becomes a person in the true sense, conscious of his duty to himself and to his fellow man.

CONCLUSION

Hedonism is correct in emphasizing that man is a sentient being. It errs, however, in maintaining that feeling or sentiency encompasses the total life of man and that his highest good is embodied in feeling alone. Feeling, after all, does not provide for its own guidance. Feeling, which is no more than the expression of animal in man, needs the guidance, the illumination of reason. Hedonism, by its one-sidedness, cannot possibly make good its claim of being the answer to man's chief good.

In Rationalism no more than in Hedonism can we expect to find the highest good in life. Reason indeed must be the governing force in man's activities. A rational self-mastery is the very essence of morality. But such a self-mastery is not effected by the withdrawal of reason from life's battle, by its retreat within the sanctuary of pure thought and undisturbed philosophical meditation. Rationalism, like Hedonism, is too simple a theory. In the one case as in the other, the form of reason without the content of feeling is empty; as the content of feeling without the form of reason is blind.

Neither in Hedonism nor in Rationalism, neither in the life of pure sensibility nor in the life of pure reason, is man's chief good to be found. If there is such a thing as a chief good in life, it lies in the harmonization of both sides of man's nature—the physical and the intellectual aspects of his being. The reconciliation of both sides of man's nature is what Eudaemonism calls for.

Of the three theories which claim to have the answer as to what may be considered as man's highest good, Eudaemonism is the one which promises balance in one's life. Few would disagree that such a life is the kind that most human beings dream of, that most would regard as man's chief good.

Part II
RELIGION

The "religious instinct" or "the religious function", or by whatever name we choose to identify it, is an integral part of human nature. Man is impelled to attach himself to some object regarded as higher than himself, and conceived of as transcendental. His speculations about this object cannot suppress his longing for it. He is forever "yearning after the infinite".

S.U.

1. Theories of the Origin of Religion

RELIGION IS UNIVERSAL

Most anthropologists concur that no people or tribe has been discovered which is without some form of religion—though it may not entirely agree with our more dignified concept of it. There are numerous accounts by Greek historians and geographers of the religions, not only of the peoples of their times, but of many barbarous tribes in all parts of the world. They report that they nowhere found men who might be regarded as irreligious.

Among the remains of paleolithic culture, there are objects which are unhesitatingly interpreted as religious. It seems that religion is universal and begins at the most primitive state of human existence.

THEORIES ON HOW RELIGION BEGAN

Even though historical investigation may trace a particular

religion to its earliest beginnings, it does not tell us how religion began in the first place. Any attempt to furnish the answer to this question must necessarily be pure speculation. It is worthwhile noting that the question did not seriously present itself to the minds of thinkers till the days of the English Deists.[46] The Greek philosophers did not concern themselves with the question, while Jewish, Christian, and Mohammedan theologians attributed the rise of religion to Divine Revelation— either a primitive form given to all mankind or a special Revelation to certain peoples. In either case, they took the position that there was a continuous Revelation of the deity.

THE THEORY OF THE ENGLISH DEISTS

The Deists held that the human intellect is the source for religion. The belief in a god, the immortality of the soul, could unshakably be established, they claimed, through the intellect. It was also their belief that this religion of reason was natural to man and therefore known to him from the beginning.

DAVID HUME'S THEORY

David Hume,[47] in his *Natural History of Religion*, rejects the factor of reason as the source of religion; instead he substitutes for it two others—fear and hope. It was man's fear of the forces of nature, he argues, that led him to seek powerful gods behind them. By a natural process he personified them, but his fear of these beings was tempered by the hope of securing their favor, and toward this end all his efforts were directed. After a long process of choosing a certain god or gods above others, he

---

[46] A movement arising in England in the 17th century and continuing through the 18th. Deism asserted belief in one God, creator of the Universe, but regarded Him as detached from the world and making no revelation.

[47] David Hume, *The Natural History of Religion* (London: Green and Grose's ed. of "Hume's Essays" 1882), Vol. II, p. 49.

finally selected the god which he believed was in control of the universe.

While Hume differs from the Deists on reason as being the chief source for religion, he is in accord with them in discounting Revelation as a factor in the rise and origin of religion.

THE THEORY OF ALBERT REVILLE

Reville,[48] in his *Prolegomena of the History of Religions*, points out that there is lack of evidence, from a historical viewpoint, for considering a Primitive Revelation to mankind. Even if Reville's argument were refuted, we should still be confronted with the problem how, if there were a Primitive Revelation, we could prove it by a historical study of religions. It is true that, in tracing religion to its earliest beginnings, we find certain beliefs and certain rites which appear to transcend the intellectual limits of primitive man, but to attribute these to a Primitive Revelation means either giving up the problem of accounting for them or accepting Primitive Revelation as a definite answer to the question.

It seems that the theory of Primitive Revelation lies beyond the scope of a historical study of religions, and this includes also a supposed "Primitive Tradition" which some scholars are inclined to substitute for Revelation.

EDWARD TYLOR'S THEORY

A theory of the origin of religion which has attracted the attention of students of religion is one which was introduced by the eminent anthropologist Edward B. Tylor[49] and which is known as the animistic theory. Tylor in his famous work, *Primitive Culture*, shows that one of the very first things which

---

[48] Albert Reville, *Prolegomena of the History of Religions* (Paris: 1881, Eng. trans. by B.S. Squire, London: 1884), p. 25.

[49] Edward B. Tylor, *Primitive Culture* (London: 1871), Chapters XI-XVII.

attracted men as they became consciously intelligent was the fact of life stirring in the world. They perceived that animals were alive much as they themselves were, that trees and plants grew and died and came to life again, that breezes blew and rains fell to revive the parched land, that the sun, moon, and stars seemed to move in the heavens, that life flourished in the sunshine and died in the dark. At first, perhaps, only everything that could move seemed to them alive; with the passing of time, however, inanimate objects such as mountains, trees, rivers, and stones were considered by them as possessed with life. Tylor believes that from all this, it is possible to derive by a natural evolutionary process all forms of worship as well as different religious doctrines. Tylor's view, because of its logic and simplicity, commended itself to a host of scholars. Yet, this theory does not exhaust the questioning mind on the subject. It cannot be denied that animism is a belief common to mankind, and may even be regarded as a definitely established thesis, but the question that is still raised and waits for an answer is whether Tylor is completely correct in assuming that animism is the earliest form of belief. We may accept the notion that animism is the earliest system of religious philosophy devised by man, but does he not perhaps devise this system until he is in a more advanced stage of culture? Primitive man might indeed reach the conclusion that the flowing river is alive, that there is life in a blossoming tree, but he is not yet sufficiently intelligent to link the life in the stone with the life in the tree and conclude that all nature is permeated with a single kind of life, manifesting itself in manifold ways.

There are those who hold that religious manifestations precede even animism, and they add that if man was without religion before the animistic theory presented itself to his mind, animism by itself would not have led to the rise of religion. It is inconceivable, they say, that trees and stones, rivers and mountains could excite man's emotions to the point of kindling in him the "divine spark." Animism as a theory for the origin of religion is not without defect.

HERBERT SPENCER'S THEORY

Another theory on the origin of religion is the one advanced by Herbert Spencer[50] who, in his *Principles of Sociology*, chapters eight to seventeen, traces the beginning of religion to Ancestor Worship. In his opinion man's fear of the spirits of his ancestors gave rise to prayer, called forth reverence, and produced religion. Spencer's theory is predicated on the idea that the gods worshipped by primitive man are the spirits of his ancestors. According to Spencer, Ancestor Worship is more primitive than nature worship. But, when the history of religion is traced to its earliest beginnings, the adoration of ghosts is not found to be as prevalent and as prominent as Spencer would have us believe. On the contrary, if animism or nature worship belongs to a more advanced period in primitive life, then a religion based on ancestral worship must be placed in an even more advanced period of ancient culture.

The fact that among the primitive peoples are found elaborate ceremonials in connection with their dead does not warrant a conclusion that ancient man's thoughts about his dead ancestors form the starting point of religion.

THE THEORY OF REVELATION THROUGH NATURE

One theory, which is not without a number of supporters, ascribes the origin of religion to a revelation of something divine in the universe made to man through nature, which, it is claimed, is so ordered as to lead even primitive man to the recognition of higher powers. This revelation, together with man's attempt to win the favor of the powers recognized by him, results in rendering man into a religious being.

In analyzing this theory, C.P. Tiele[51] points out its weakness.

---

[50] Herbert Spencer, *Principles of Sociology* (London: 1862), Chapters viii-xvii.

[51] C.P. Tiele, *Elements of the Science of Religion* (Edinburgh: 1897), Vol. I, pp. 43-45; Vol. II, p. 211.

He is in agreement with the first part of the proposition, the revelation of nature to man. But the second part of the proposition, he says, does not fully account for man's endeavor to put himself into proper relations with the powers recognized by him. This, after all, is the religious element in man, and the question as to the origin of religion is answered only when we have discovered how man came to possess an element in his being which made him receptive to religious influences in the first place. Tiele rejects this theory as the answer to the question of how religion began.

THE THEORY OF MAX F. MÜLLER

Perhaps the most logical theory on the origin of religion has been propounded by Max Müller. According to Müller,[52] man from the very beginning is possessed with a spiritual element, which he terms as "the perception of the Infinite"—or, as the Psalmist has it, the yearning of the soul after God. This perception, Müller believes, comes to life in man, primitive or advanced, when he thinks of his insignificance against—not any part of nature, but the sum-total that he finds outside of his being—and is overwhelmed by it. Müller does not assume that at the outset of his primitive life man could give a clear account to himself of his "perception of the Infinite." Yet, he strongly believes that his "perception" is sufficient in order to leave a lasting impression upon his soul. Once the thought of the Infinite has taken hold of man it never leaves him. He is conscious of it during his every waking moment, and as he grows intellectually it grows in meaning for him. In the light of Müller's theory, we see that man's fear of nature, his personification of it, and his reverence for it are only symbols reflecting something deep in his soul which embraces the totality of the universe and its mystery, which he eventually calls God.

---

[52]   Max F. Müller, *On the Origin and Growth of Religion* (London: 1880).

2. Mythology and Man's Myth-Making Faculty

THE CHARACTER AND FUNCTION OF A MYTH

I t is not easy to define a myth; but practically all myths appear to possess certain characteristics in common. Myths are traditional; this means that they originate in a "mythological age," which reflects a particular stage in the development of human thought. A myth differs from other tales in that it is believed to be substantially true by those among whom it is first repeated. The purpose of most myths is to explain certain phenomena, beliefs, or customs. Thus there is a connection between mythology and theology or religion. The function of myth is to bolster tradition, give it greater value and prestige by tracing it back to a higher, better, more supernatural reality of ancient events.

Mythology is intertwined with the religion of primitive man, and it is safe to say that mythical elements are included in the religion of modern man. It may almost be considered a truism that a myth-making faculty is the common possession of humanity.

125

By our acquaintance with the mythology of a people we are offered a glimpse of some phases of their religious beliefs, particularly the beliefs of the masses. For it is the popular mind that generally reveals itself in the myths.

MYTH AND PRIMITIVE MAN

Myth forms the natural medium for primitive man in giving expression to his thoughts about natural phenomena. The roar of the thunder, for example, flashes of lightning, the constant change of night and day, the changes of the seasons, or such rarer occurrences as eclipses of the sun or moon prompt him to seek an explanation for all this. The explanation that he gives to his questions results in the formation of nature myths.

Nature myths are the result of primitive man's personification of the natural powers whose manifestations he witnesses. The storm he personifies as a huge bird; the sun he regards as a human being; the sun and moon he imagines as husband and wife or brother and sister, or two rival rulers; the lightning he regards as a dragon.[53]

Ascribing life to all things is an axiom of primitive man's science, and since the only life about which he knows anything is that which he witnesses in himself, in his fellows, and in the animals about him, the powers of nature he likewise conceives as animate beings—either in human or animal shape. Of course, the objects primitive man selects for personification vary and differ on account of climatic conditions and habits of life.

THE INFLUENCE OF MYTHOLOGY AND RELIGION

While myths have their origin in an early period of history and have strong meaning and appeal for the age in which they

---

[53] For examples see Andrew Lang's *Myth, Ritual and Religion* (London, 1887; 2nd ed., 1899).

are produced, yet we find that the more sophisticated ages of man continue to create myth. How do we account for it? What explanation is there for an intelligent Greek, a contemporary of Sophocles, accepting literally the stories told of Zeus or Aphrodite or Apollo? The only answer we can give to the question is that the hoary antiquity of the tales about the gods lent to them an almost sacred character. Had it not been for the Greek beliefs in the reality of the gods described in the myths, the belief in them would have been undermined long before the advent of Christianity.

The Greeks knew nothing of a time when the stories about their gods did not exist, hence their skepticism did not go beyond an attempt at removing those features from the myths which appeared objectionable to their age—features which in their estimation pictured the gods on a moral level lower than that reached by human beings. The tales, the Greeks maintained, had originally a different import, but as far as they were concerned, they could not doubt that they were without some meaning for them.

MYTH REINFORCED BY LITERARY FORM

The belief that the myths responded to some kind of reality was reinforced by the literary form given to them. The beauty and charm of Homer were too powerful to be resisted, and people could not bring themselves to believe that what had inspired a mortal to such wonderful flights should turn out to be nothing more than human fancy, no more than a mass of idle tales.

The same may be said of the hymns of the Rig-Veda, which were even more precious to the people of India than Homer's poems were to the Greeks. The beliefs expressed in the hymns and the advanced ideas of the people recorded in other compositions which were free from mythical tradition showed inconsistency of belief, but this was ignored. The gap between ancient popular conceptions and later concepts continued to widen, and ultimately resulted in new forms of faith which corresponded to the new religious conditions. Yet, even in the new forms much of the old mythology survived.

There can be no doubt that the incorporation of myths in literary form gave them a sacred significance which perpetuated them and strengthened belief in them.

When a people reaches a level in its religious thought, and its mythology is no longer adequate for the level reached, conflict generally ensues and the result which follows is compromise. The old tales are carried over into the higher forms of the religion and are so reinterpreted as to make them correspond to the new order of thought. The myth, then, in lieu of being a theory of primitive science, becomes a poetic symbol conveying ethical ideas.

PHILOSOPHY AND MYTH

Philosophy also plays an important role in preserving myth. It injects a new meaning into it by eliminating its objectionable features, thus making it more acceptable for the age in which its old meaning is no longer acceptable. Finally, when mythology in its most diluted form can no longer appeal to the imagination of the people, and can no longer be incorporated in the body of a people's religion, then some of the more popular myths are transferred to favored individuals who have no connection with the myths, but who lend themselves to this species of adaptation. At this point, myths assume the character of religious legends. There is hardly a great figure to be found in the religions of Judaism, Christianity, and Islam whose life has not been embroidered with an ancient myth in the guise of a legend.

DOES MYTHOLOGY WEAKEN RELIGION?

Since mythology is so interwoven with the fabric of religion, and since it is no more than pure fiction, does it not weaken the reality of religious truth? The answer to the question is no, because religion does not deal with scientific truth. Religion caters to man's emotions, and where the emotions come into play the intellect recedes into the background. This explains why mythology with its appeal to the emotions, instead of weakening religion, strengthens and supports it.

3. Who Is a Mystic and What Is Mysticism?

WHO IS A MYSTIC?

A mystic is one who is consumed by a belief that the world which he experiences through his senses is a mere veil which hides from him the Real World. Penetrating this veil, by which he feels separated from True Reality, is his paramount concern and highest objective.

But what is it that leads the mystic to the belief that there is something beyond, something more than what his senses report to him of the familiar world? The mystic is convinced that in addition to his senses man possesses an inner light, a level of consciousness by which he can transcend materiality and thereby make contact with the Soul of the universe or, as Ralph Waldo Emerson termed it, "The Over Soul."

Stated in another way, the mystic believes in the possibility of direct intercourse with the Being of beings, not through revelations, rituals, prayers, or other such media. God, to the mystic, ceases to be an object and becomes an experience.

WHAT IS MYSTICISM?

From what we know of mystics, we can say that mysticism is the immediate consciousness of God, the direct experience of religious truth.

Mysticism, says Rufus Jones, "is an immediate, intuitive knowledge of God...or of transcendent Reality or of Divine Presence."[54]

In the words of Evelyn Underhill, "Mysticism is not an opinion; it is not a philosophy. It has nothing in common with the pursuit of occult knowledge. On the one hand, It is not merely the power of contemplating Eternity; on the other, it is not to be identified with any religious queerness. It is the name of that organic process which involves the perfect consummation of the Love of God; the achievement here and now of the immortal heritage of man, or, if you like it better, for this means the same thing—it is the art of establishing his conscious relation with the Absolute."[55]

SOURCE OF THE MYSTICAL FACULTY

Mysticism views the essence of life and the world as an all-embracing spiritual substance and the human personality as a duality. One aspect of human nature, mysticism asserts, is the result of its relation with the material objects of the universe, contacted by the senses. The other aspect of human nature is derived from its participation in the universal spiritual substance of life. Now, as man's bodily senses keep him informed of the world of matter, so that higher aspect of his nature which acts as intermediary between the Supreme Universal Reality and his circumscribed person is endowed with the faculty which makes him aware of the modalities of the

---

[54] Rufus M. Jones, *The Flowering of Mysticism* (New York: Hafner Publishing Co., 1971), p. 25.

[55] Evelyn Underhill, *Mysticism* (New York: E.P. Dutton Co., 1961), p. 81.

transcendent realm to which it pertains. This is held to be the source of the mystical faculty.

Each aspect of man's nature is directed toward the particular area whence it derives its being and thrives in proportion to the amount of attention and interest it receives from the individual. Thus, the mystic finds it necessary to subdue his earthly concerns, desires, and appetites in order to enable his spiritual faculties to develop to the point of becoming conscious of belonging to or of entering the realm of spiritual Unity.

MYSTICISM AND INTUITION

Mysticism, like philosophy, arises from the elemental human desire to search and investigate both natural and spiritual phenomena, and to understand their manifestations more thoroughly. But, while philosophy relies mainly on human reason and accepts it as the standard, mysticism, which is permeated with the emotional religious feeling inherent in man, is, in addition to reason, actuated by intuition, a concept through which mystics believe direct and immediate truth is achieved.

Henri Bergson (1869-1949) protests against the excessive tribute paid to intellect, or intelligence, and to science as the ripest fruit of intelligence. Intelligence, according to Bergson, has for its original function the construction and use of inorganic tools in the service of life. It is, therefore, most at home in the world of inert solids. Now, for the practical purpose of making tools it is convenient to treat material bodies as discrete units each divisible *ad libitum*. But when intelligence becomes theoretical, and seeks to explain life and thought as well as inert matter, then it leads astray. For it tends to treat all things as if they consisted of lifeless matter, and the whole of reality is reduced to a dead mechanism, for intelligence is unable to comprehend life.

This defect of intelligence must be made good by intuition, which can reveal the most intimate secrets of life. Intuition, according to Bergson, leads us to the very inwardness of life as successfully as intelligence guides us into the secrets of matter. Human consciousness is predominantly intellectual. But man is not entirely lacking in intuition, which functions whenever our deepest interests are at stake.[56]

STAGES TOWARD THE MYSTICAL EXPERIENCE

There seems to prevail a general method employed by mystics of all races and all faiths by which they are led from the experience of the sensory world of separate objects to a new world of unity in which the mystical experience is realized. This method consists of three different stages leading to the final experience. First, there is the purgative stage—which involves the preliminary elimination of worldly interests and the eradication of the passions originating from them.

The second stage toward the mystical experience is attained when the soul has succeeded in detaching itself from the coarse appetites and the allurements of materiality and reaches a degree of increased enlightenment and inner freedom.

The last stage toward the mystical experience is achieved when the battle against the earthly nature is won, and the union between the mystic and the divine object of his quest takes place.

THE MYSTICAL EXPERIENCE

Mystical experience is not limited to any one particular race or one particular people. It is undoubtedly one of the original grounds of personal religion. Mystical experience is marked by the emergence of a type of consciousness which is not sharply differentiated into a subject-object state. The "subject" and "object" are fused into an undivided one. Whatever is seen,

[56] See Henri Bergson, *Introduction to Metaphysics* (New York: Philosophical Library, 1961).

heard, or felt in mystical moments is flooded with an inrush from the depths of the inner life. The individual soul feels invaded, vitalized with new energy, liberated and exalted with a sense of having found what it has always dreamed of.

THE MYSTIC WAY

Mysticism is completely an activity of the spirit. "The spirit of the mystic," says Johannes Tauler, "is as it were sunk and lost in the Abyss of the Deity, and loses the consciousness of all creature distinctions. All things are gathered together in one with the divine sweetness, and the man's being is so penetrated with the divine substance that he loses himself therein, as a drop of water is lost in a cask of strong wine. And thus the man's spirit is so sunk in God in divine union, that he loses all sense of distinction...and there remains a secret, still union, without a cloud of color."[57]

The mystic's most distinctive mark is love. His love is expressed in a deep-seated desire of his soul toward its Source. God, say the mystics, cannot be known by reason but only by the love of one's heart. The mystic seeks to surrender himself to ultimate Reality, not for any personal gain, worldly joys, but purely from an instance of love. The mystic is in love with the Absolute.

Spiritual desires are useless, the mystics claim, unless the whole self is properly conditioned and directed toward the Real. The Mystic Way is a trying psychological and spiritual process which entails "the remaking of character and the liberation of a new, or rather latent, form of consciousness; which imposes on the self the condition which is sometimes called 'ecstasy' but is better named the Unitive State."[58]

---

[57] Johannes Tauler, *Sermon for Septuagesima Sunday*, Susanna Winkworth's trans. (London: 1906), p. 253.

[58] Evelyn Underhill, *Mysticism*, p. 81.

BELIEFS OF MYSTICISM

Mysticism is characterized by certain beliefs. One belief of mysticism is in a way of wisdom that is sudden, penetrating, independent of the senses.

A second belief of mysticism is that of unity. It rejects the idea of division anywhere.

A third belief of mysticism is that time is unreal. This belief flows from its belief of unity or its rejection of division. If all is one, then the idea of past and future is unreal.

HOW THE MYSTIC DIFFERS FROM THE ORDINARY RELIGIONIST

The mystic differs from the ordinary religionist in that, whereas the latter knows God through an objective revelation, whether in nature or as embodied in the Bible (which is really only secondhand knowledge, mediate, external, the record of other people's visions and experiences), the mystic knows God by contact of spirit with spirit. He has the immediate vision; he hears the "still small voice" speaking clearly to him in the silence of his soul. In this sense the mystic stands quite outside the field of all the great religions of the world. Religion to him is merely his own individual religion, his own lonely, isolated quest for truth. He is solitary, a soul alone with God.

Upon examining the lives and works of mystics, however, we usually find that in spite of the intensely individualistic type of their religion, they are related to some particular religion of the world's religions. Their mystical experiences are colored and molded by some dominant faith. The specific forms of their conceptions of God do not come from their own inner light only, but from the teachings which they absorb from the external and traditional religion of their race or country. Thus, there is Jewish Mysticism, Christian Mysticism, Islamic Mysticism,

Buddhist Mysticism, Hindu Mysticism, etc. The goal that each type stresses, however, is the same for all mystics.

MYSTICISM AND FREEDOM

The mystic, of all the people in the world, enjoys genuine and complete freedom. The freedom of the mystic is derived from his inner being. He achieves it by detaching himself from things material, external, from pursuing those things which promise much but in the end offer nothing but emptiness, disillusionment, and disappointment.

The mystic knows that man's desire for things is never quelled. He forever remains hungry. No matter how much he has, he wants more and more. And in his drive to gain more, newer, and better things, he is always in a state of restlessness and disturbance. His goal is never met; it continuously recedes; his pursuit after it, ends only when his life does. No one has ever declared that he has attained serenity of spirit, inner freedom, as a result of his material treasures.

"In detachment," says St. John of the Cross, "the spirit finds quiet and repose for coveting nothing.... For as soon as it covets anything, it is immediately fatigued thereby."[59]

Once an individual succeeds in transcending his cravings for materiality—that which promises and does not fulfill, that which allures and ultimately ensnares and enslaves—the downward drag is at an end. "Then a free spirit in a free world, the self moves upon its true orbit; undistracted by the largely self-imposed needs and demands of ordinary earthly existence."[60] This free spirit, which may be termed as the redeemed self, is that of the mystic. He alone knows the meaning of inner peace and freedom in its deepest sense.

---

[59] St. John of the Cross, *The Ascent of Mt. Carmel*, trans. by D. Lewis, new ed. (London: 1906), Bk. I, chap. xiii.

[60] Evelyn Underhill, *Mysticism*, p. 207.

HOW NON-MYSTICS VIEW THE MYSTICS

In his famous *Allegory of the Cave*, Plato presents two aspects of reality. He describes a race of people who for several centuries were confined to a cave. In this cave, they could see nothing but the shadows of images projected against the wall of the cave as they passed along a ledge between the wall and a fire. Reality to them consisted of the shadows, for that was all they had been accustomed to seeing.

One day a young man received permission to leave the cave. As he approached its mouth he was repulsed by the bright light of the sun. He waited until evening and then went forth into the outside world. He found that even the light of the moon and stars was too strong for his weakened eyes. After some time, when his vision improved, he began to notice the beauty and splendor that surrounded him. For a while he could not believe that the world he was seeing was real, but he soon began to realize that, instead of it being unreal, it was rather the shadows of the cave that in fact were empty of meaning and reality. Wishing to share his incredible experience with his compatriots whom he left behind, he therefore returned to the cave. By this time, he no longer possessed the capacity to tolerate the darkness or see any meaning in the shadows. When he began to relate to his fellow prisoners the wonders and magnificence of the outside world, they mocked him and considered him mad. The outside world, they concluded, caused him to lose both his sight and his mind. They resolved that, in the future, any one of them who would attempt to leave the cave, forsake the security of the real world for the illusion of that outside world, would be severely punished.[61]

Plato's allegory indirectly portrays the attitude of the non-mystic toward the mystic. Like the young man of the cave, who discovers true reality outside of it, the mystic discovers a reality

---

[61] Plato, *The Republic*, VII, 514a-521b; *Great Dialogues of Plato*, trans. W.H.D. Rouse (New York: New American Library, 1960).

independent of the senses. But when he reports his discovery to his fellow men whose lives are grounded in the sense world, whose spirituality lies dormant in them, they listen to his tale of excitement with suspicion, and think of him as having lost his way.

THE VALUE OF STUDYING THE LIFE OF THE MYSTIC

From the study of the life of the mystic, we gain a deeper understanding of him as well as of ourselves. We learn that his struggle for true Reality is an effort on his part to transcend the sense world, escape its bondage, achieve a higher level of consciousness, and ultimately shift his center of interest from the natural to the spiritual plane.

Our study further impresses upon us the thought that the spring of amazing energy which enables the mystic to rise to inner freedom and dominate his world, is latent in all of us and is an integral part of our humanity; that the mystic's achievements can also be ours if we were to choose to go his way, make similar sacrifices by forsaking what he considers as the illusory world, which is responsible for our restlessness, for that which he considers as the Real World, which gives him inner peace.

4. The Zen Way

THE MEANING OF THE TERM ZEN

Zen is the Japanese counterpart of the Chinese word *ch'an*, which in turn is a translation of the Sanskrit word *dhyana*, meaning the meditation that leads to insight.

ORIGIN OF ZEN

Within the century of Buddha's death, Buddhism divided itself into two separate schools. Each called itself a *yana*, a raft or ferry, for each proposed to carry man across the sea of life to the shore of enlightenment. In the course of time one school took the name of Mahayana, the Big Raft, and the other adopted the name of Hinayana, or the Little Raft. Not pleased with this name, the Hinayanists changed their name to Theravada or the Way of the Elders.

The members of the Theravada school base their beliefs on

139

the teachings of Buddha as recorded in the earliest texts, those of the Pali Canon. The Mahayanists place emphasis on Buddha's life instead of his teachings.

The ideal type as projected by the two schools differ markedly. The Theravadin ideal is the perfected disciple who through intense concentration and will makes his way toward Nirvana (the eternal, hidden, and incomprehensible peace).

The Mahayana ideal is "one whose essence is perfected wisdom," a being who, having brought himself to the brink of Nirvana, renounces his prize that he may return to the world to make it accessible to others.

The difference between the two types is illustrated in the story of four men who, journeying across an immense desert, came upon a compound surrounded by high walls. One of the four determines to find out what is inside. He scales the wall and on reaching the top gives a whoop of delight and jumps over. The second and third do likewise. When the fourth man gets to the top of the wall, he sees below him an enchanted garden with sparkling streams, pleasant groves, and delicious fruit. Though longing to jump over, he resists the impulse. Remembering other wayfarers who are trudging through the burning desert, he climbs back down and devotes himself to directing them to the oasis. The first three may be classified as Theravadins. The last one may be described as a Mahayanist. He vows not to desert the world "until grass itself be enlightened." This, of course, was Buddha's consuming interest in his life and it is the same for the Mahayanists who attempt to follow his example.

Theravada Buddhism centers on monks. Monasteries are the spiritual focus of the lands where it predominates (Ceylon, Burma, Thailand, and Cambodia). Renunciation of the world is held in high national esteem, and even men who do not intend to become monks for their entire lives are expected to live as such for a year or two so that their lives may take on some of the monastic virtues.

Mahayana Buddhism is primarily a religion for laymen. Even its priests are expected to make the service of laymen their primary concern. Its popularity is far greater than that of Theravada. Mahayana has its followers in Mongolia, Tibet, China, Korea, and Japan.

Due to the liberal attitude of Mahayana toward variation, it split into five main schools. One stresses faith, another study, a third relies on efficacious formulas, a fourth assumes a semi-political tint, and the fifth, which appears in its most alive form in Japan today, is the Mahayana intuitive school and is known as Zen Buddhism.

Zen Buddhists, like other Mahayanists, trace their perspective back to Gautama—Buddha himself. His teachings that were incorporated in the Pali Canon, they held, were those the masses seized upon. His more perceptive followers, they maintain, caught from their master a higher angle of vision. As an example of their deeper understanding of Buddha's message, they refer to his Flower Sermon—which, according to tradition, he delivered from the top of a mountain without the use of words. He simply held aloft a golden lotus. Among those who stood around him only one—by the name of Mahakasyapas—smiled, indicating that he had gotten the point. Gautama designated him as his successor. The insight that prompted Mahakasyapas to smile was transmitted in India through Twenty-Eight Patriarchs and carried to China in 521 A.D. by Bodhidharma. From there it spread to Japan in the Twelfth Century—bringing to it the secret of Zen.

WHAT IS ZEN?

Like Existentialism, Zen is an attitude toward life; more precisely, it is a way of life. As a way of life, Zen's chief aim is to face life head on. Life, according to Zen, is not to be theorized, intellectualized, talked about, thought about, but confronted, embraced, and lived. It is to be taken hold of, so to speak, with bare hands.

The more one thinks about life, Zen indicates, the more one raises questions about it, the more confused he becomes. Zen concerns itself with facts. Such questions as to the possibility of life after death, whether or not there is a heaven or hell, are in Zen's view best left alone. These are questions to which there are no ultimate answers. Zen is everyday thought, everyday action. Zen is everyday life. In its essence, Zen is the art of seeing into one's being and discovering the powers with which to confront life.

According to Daisetz Teitaro Suzuki (1870-1906), the famous Buddhist scholar, Zen consists of acquiring a fresh viewpoint for looking at life and things generally. This is done, Suzuki claims, by abandoning our ordinary habits of thinking which dominate our everyday life.

The acquiring of a new point of view in our dealings with life and the world, is popularly called by Japanese Zen students Satori, which is another name for enlightenment.

Satori may be defined as an insight, an intuitive looking into the nature of things in contradistinction to the analytical or logical understanding of it. It is not a kind of insight or attitude toward life that emerges as the end of a process of reasoning. It is not the result of a series of inference. The Satori involves a leap into a level of experience different from that of a conceptual type. Practically, it means the experiencing of a world hitherto unexperienced. With Satori our entire surroundings are viewed from quite an unexpected angle of perception. The world for those who have gained a Satori is no longer the old world as it used to be.

THE INTELLECT AND ZEN

To comprehend Zen is a trying task. It requires the reordering of one's way of looking at things—that is, viewing them from the inside rather than the outside, superficially. Zen cannot be attained before one rids himself of the notion that the intellect can be called upon to solve life's problems as it solves problems of science and mathematics.

Zen does not minimize the importance of intellect as such. What it wishes us to understand is that the intellect has its limitations. It objects to our dependence on the intellect as the main source from which one can obtain answers to any question that is raised. For we often raise questions that are beyond the power of the intellect to answer.

Even though the intellect has the capacity of probing the mysteries of life, nevertheless we should not expect satisfaction from it when the questions relate to our being itself. Such questions which pertain to being itself, according to Zen, emerge from the depths of our consciousness, which are beyond the reach of the intellect. The intellect, Zen stresses, is only the periphery of our being.

If the intellect serves as an obstacle for the attainment of Zen, by what means then can it be attained? The way to Zen, say the Zen masters, is through intuition and will.

ZEN IS A PERSONAL EXPERIENCE

Zen defies description. It cannot be conveyed by word of mouth. It cannot be taught. It is purely a direct personal experience. There is no way the outsider, the curious, can gain an inkling of what Zen is except by following closely the questions the Zen aspirant asks of his Master and the Master's reply.

The questions that are generally asked by the Zen aspirant are of the type that the average person would ask. The answers that are given appear on the surface to be abrupt, insulting, harsh, and ofttimes illogical and confusing. The reason for this is to help the questioner realize that, if he repeated the question to himself, he would soon have the answer to his question, or would quickly realize that his question is so nonsensical that it is not deserving of an answer, or that in actuality there is no answer to the question posed.

The following questions asked by Zen aspirants of their Masters and the answers that are given should afford the curious some idea of what Zen is about.

ON REGARDING THE SOUL AS AN OBJECT

A monk pleads, saying to his Master, "O Master, pacify my soul!" The Master replies, "Bring me your soul and I will pacify it." "But Master," says the monk, "I have searched and struggled and have been unable to find my soul." The reply of the Master is, "Your soul is already pacified."

ON PREOCCUPYING ONESELF WITH THE INCONSEQUENTIAL

A monk asks, "Master, what is my self?" and the Master replies, "What would you do with a self if you had one?"

ON THE FUTILITY OF THEORIZING

A group of monks were engaged in a philosophical dispute concerning a fluttering pennant which was on a pole in the monastery courtyard. One monk argued that, since the pennant is an inanimate object, it is the wind that makes it flap. Another gave the view that the wind is also inanimate, so the flapping is due to a certain combination of causes and conditions. A third proposed the theory that there is no flapping pennant, but the wind moving by itself. When the Master came along he was asked to give his opinion. He remarked, "It is neither wind nor the pennant that is flapping, but your minds."

ATTEMPTING TO ESCAPE REALITY

A monk asks, "Master, summer comes, winter comes, how shall we escape it?" "Why not go to a place where there is neither summer nor winter?" is the Master's reply. "But," says the monk, "where can such a place be found?" The Master's response is, "When winter comes you shiver, when summer comes you sweat."

ON ACCEPTING THE DAILY ROUTINE OF LIFE

A Master was once asked, "We have to dress and eat every day; how can we escape all that?" The Master replied, "We dress, we eat." And when the monk complained, "I do not understand you," the Master said to him, "If you don't understand, put on your robe and eat your food."

THE NEED OF EXPERIENCING LIFE DIRECTLY

While walking over a bridge stretching over the Zen River, a monk asked his Master as to the depth of the river. The Master seized the monk and would have thrown him down into the rapids had not his friends hurriedly interceded for him. The Master wanted the questioner himself to go down to the bottom of Zen and survey its depths according to his own measure.

ASKING WHAT ZEN IS ABOUT IS ASKING WHAT LIFE IS ABOUT

A monk once approached a Zen Master and asked to be enlightened on Zen. The Master told him to come when nobody was around. When the monk appeared before the Master when he was alone and repeated his request, the Master asked him to come closer, and when the monk did as told, the

Master whispered to him, "Zen is something that cannot be conveyed by word of mouth."

EXPECTING SENSIBLE ANSWERS TO NONSENSICAL QUESTIONS

A monk says to his Master, "Yesterday you declared that the whole universe is one transpicuous crystal; how am I to understand that?" The Master replies, "The whole universe is one transpicuous crystal, and what is the sense of understanding it?"

A monk asked the Master to play him a tune on a stringless harp. The Master was silent a few moments, and then said, "There, do you hear it?" And when the monk replied, "Alas, no, Master!" the Master reproached him with, "Why didn't you ask me to play louder?"

ON CONFUSING SYMBOL WITH SUBSTANCE

"A basket is welcome to carry our fish home," Suzuki says, "but when the fish are safely on the table why should we eternally bother ourselves with the basket?"

THE PURPOSE OF THE ZEN DIALOGUES

The purpose of the dialogues between the monk and the Master is to enable us to see ourselves as others see us, hear ourselves as others hear us, and to make us realize that life must be accepted as it presents itself, that we must go about doing our daily tasks and desist expecting from life what it cannot give.

To put it another way, the dialogues serve as a double mirror. One is held up against life, and the other against ourselves—looking at life.

ZEN'S MESSAGE

The message of Zen is that there is no escaping from life. This truth Zen tries to bring home by the following parable: There was an old woman who was born at the same time as the Buddha, and they lived in the same place throughout their lives. The old woman did not want to see the Buddha; whenever he came near she did all she could to avoid him, running here and there to hide herself. But one day, finding it impossible to run away, she covered her face with her hands—and lo! the Buddha appeared between each of her ten fingers.

The Zen solution to the great problem of life, Suzuki pointed out, is not attempting to solve it at all: "The not solving is really the solving." By this he no doubt meant that it is futile to seek a solution to the problem of life because there is no solution. Once one accepts life as it really is, as fact, then the problem is eliminated from his mind. In an indirect, subtle way, Zen drives home the lesson that life is to be lived and not philosophized.

5. The Purpose and Power of Yoga

U nlike the philosophers of ancient Greece, who directed their minds to the exploration of the outer world, the physical world, the philosophers of India, thousands of years ago, focused on the inner world of man.

The interest and concern of Western philosophy in the course of time gave rise to science and technology. The concentration of the Indic sages on the nature of man, his inner being, his latent powers, promoted their understanding of his spirit, his soul's deepest longing, which in their view is to unite with the Soul of the universe.

To help man achieve this end, the wise men of India devised certain methods for man to follow, which are known as Yogas.

THE WORD YOGA

The word *Yoga* comes from the same root as the English

word Yoke—and it means to bring together or unite. Yoga actually is a method of training, designed to help man in the linking of his soul with the Godhead, or the Supreme Soul.

TYPES OF YOGA

Of the various forms of Yoga that are prevalent in India, four are most commonly used. These are:
1. Jnana Yoga
2. Bhakti Yoga
3. Karma Yoga
4. Raja Yoga

THE AIM OF YOGA

The aim of each Yoga is the same. Why, then, are four different ones recommended? According to Hindu philosophers there are four types of individuals. One type is basically reflective, a second one primarily emotional, a third one is essentially active, and a fourth one is characterized as empirical or experimental. For each of these types of individuals a particular Yoga is recommended and designed for the development of the endowments at his disposal. However, since no man is solely reflective, emotional, active, or experimental, Hinduism encourages individuals to test all four and combine them as best suits their predilections.

JNANA YOGA

Jnana Yoga is intended for spiritual aspirants who have a strong intellectual bent. The purpose of this Yoga, or method, is to enable one to attain undying bliss and a cessation of misery through the perception of the illusoriness of names and forms, and the realization of the sole reality of Brahman, which is identical with the human soul. The follower of this path must possess keen power of reasoning, by which he can distinguish the unreal from the real, the unchanging from the changeful. He must also develop indomitable will power to detach himself from the unreal and the changing. He cultivates such disciplines as have sway over the mind and the senses, and which lead to inner calmness, forbearance, faith, and concentration. Above all, he must have an intense longing for freedom through the Knowledge of Truth.

Such an aspirant betakes himself to a qualified teacher and is instructed about the identity of the soul and Brahman. He reasons about this instruction and then contemplates its meaning. Through uninterrupted contemplation for a long time he at last attains an exalted state of superconsciousness in which he realizes oneness with Brahman.

BHAKTI YOGA

For the emotional type, Hinduism prescribes Bhakti Yoga, the path of divine love. The aspirant on this path is called a devotee or lover of God. The devotee establishes with God a human relationship, regarding Him as his Father, Master, Friend, or Beloved, according to his prevailing mood. A true devotee does not worship God because he is afraid of punishment after death or because he expects happiness on earth or in heaven.

Because the loving principle in man is directed toward unworthy self-seeking purposes, the divine harmony and felicity latent in man's heart is destroyed. By abandoning all narrow and self-centered affections, man allows the divine love to assert itself pure and unalloyed in his interior universe.

Formal and ritualistic devotion, practiced for a long time with sincerity and earnestness, is gradually transformed into spontaneous and ecstatic love, which destroys all the impurities of the devotee's heart. In other words, the devotee realizes the aim of his quest, which is reaching unity with the "Over Soul" or Brahman.

KARMA YOGA

For the active type Hinduism prescribes Karma Yoga, or the method of right activity. The aspirant must perform every action regarding himself as God's instrument. He must surrender to God all the fruits of his actions, whether philanthropic, ritualistic, or those he performs every day for the maintenance of his body. A true Karma Yogi serves others, seeing in them a manifestation of God. He regards with holy indifference success and failure and the good and bad results of his action. He cultivates a spirit of detachment from all worldly objects. To him every work is a form of worship and therefore sacred. He maintains an inner calmness being aware of his indissoluble relationship with God. Through the performance of action in the spirit of Yoga, the aspirant purifies his mind and ultimately attains the Knowledge of God and union with Him.

RAJA YOGA

Raja Yoga is intended for an individual of scientific bent. It is based on the idea of the soul being pure consciousness. Through right knowledge, Raja Yoga helps the soul realize its isolation from matter and attain freedom and perfection.

Raja Yoga prescribes the practical principles by which the soul can detach itself from matter and realize its freedom. The Raja Yoga discipline consists of eight steps. The first two deal mainly with ethical principles, such as non-injury, truthfulness, continence, contentment, study of Scripture, and devotion to God. The third and fourth describe postures and breathing which are supposed to help in the practice of concentration and meditation, given in the remaining steps.

Through the practice of ethical disciplines the aspirant gradually weakens his violent desires, which disturb the surface of his mind. It is his mental agitation that prevents an individual from experiencing his inmost self. Through concentration, the aspirant strengthens his mind and cultivates inwardness of spirit. Through the one-pointed mind he practices contemplation, analyzes the different layers of consciousness, and at last realizes the true nature of his soul and its freedom from matter. He then feels touched by the higher spheres of the life of the world, and begins to commune, as it were, with the deepest mysteries of the universe. He begins to feel as being part of the Infinite.

YOGA'S DEMANDS

Yoga makes severe demands on the one who desires to become a Yogi, a practicer of Yoga. Yoga demands the individual's fullest concentration and energy, all his thoughts, all his feelings. It demands that the individual strive to harmonize himself, to achieve inner unity, direct all his powers to serve one aim. At the same time, Yoga helps him by its method to achieve his aim.

THE EFFECT OF YOGA ON THE STUDENT

The effect of Yoga on its practicer is phenomenal. He begins to experience his life and life around him in an incredible manner. What appeared to him to be true, he now regards as false. In old ideas, he begins to discover much that he overlooked before. New horizons open before him. He looks back on his life and sees how wrongly he acted on numerous occasions, how much energy he wasted on useless pursuits. Above all, he begins to see himself in a new light. The powers that were latent in him rise to the surface. He sees not only what he is, but what he can become. His consciousness is raised to a miraculous level; his whole life undergoes a complete transformation. He begins to understand the true purpose of his existence. He feels as if he had moved into a new world, not one of illusion but one that is truly real. His heart's deepest longing, which is to overcome finitude, is fulfilled. His soul merges with the Soul of the universe.

ON BECOMING A YOGI

Anyone who wishes to study Yoga and become a Yogi should not expect to realize his wish if he limits his undertaking to reading books on the subject. The written word cannot possibly convey to the aspirant the practical knowledge he requires. What the aspirant needs in the study of Yoga is a teacher whose constant and incessant watch over him is imperative. How the pupil will fare in his work depends upon the work of the teacher upon him, and on his own indefatigable work upon himself.

HINDUISM AND BRAHMAN

As indicated above, in every instance of the practice of Yoga, the aspirant's chief concern is to achieve unity with Brahman. A description of how Hinduism views Brahman is therefore appropriate at this point.

According to Hinduism, Brahman is the Godhead or Ultimate Reality. Brahman is sometimes referred to as He and sometimes as It. Brahman is regarded as Spirit and consciousness, the unchanging Reality behind the changing universe. It is viewed both as transcendent and immanent. The world with all its forms and material objects is rooted in Reality. Material objects appear real because the Godhead, which is the only Reality, forms the inmost essence of all. By realizing It, man is released from the bondage created by ignorance. It is the essence of love. It is the essence of beauty. Physical beauty is only a reflection in matter of the beauty of the Spirit. The Godhead does not punish or reward. Man alone is responsible for his suffering and his happiness.

Hinduism declares that Brahman is unknown and unknowable. Man thinks of It according to his inner understanding. To some, It appears as the Creator of the world, the efficient cause and the giver of rewards and punishments. To others, more advanced intellectually, It is the Power manifest in the universe, the Soul of all souls. Brahman is the whole and living beings are parts of It. And to those few who have attained the highest stage of spiritual development, Brahman, soul, and the universe are one.

6. Hasidism—Its Founder and Its Principles

Victor Hugo was right in his belief that nothing is so powerful in this world as an idea whose time has come. Repeatedly in history this truth has been confirmed. Hasidism is one of those ideas whose time had come.

The Hebrew word from which the term Hasidism is derived means "the pious." Hasidism was a revolt in the eighteenth century, among the Jews of Eastern Europe, against the excessive casuistry of the contemporary rabbis. It was a protest of an emotional, uneducated people against a one-sided expression of Judaism, which they did not understand and which excluded the play of feelings and affections so that religion was made almost impossible for them.

Religion can be a source of solace, strength, and promise during trying times, as it proved to be for the Jews in their long and tragic history. For the poor, ignorant Jews, in the wild foothills of the Carpathian mountains, in the Ukraine, Judaism, as it was presented to them by their rabbis, lost its force and appeal. It was too dry, too intellectual, void of the solace and comfort that was so urgent at that time. Besides the daily morsel of bread, there was little else for which the masses could hope—crushed as they were between the restive serfs and the grasping Polish lords. That their lot would be improved by the advent of the Messiah no longer inspired them, since his coming no longer seemed real to them. And the hope that they would be rewarded in the hereafter also faded. For how could they expect to face the Almighty without a mastery of His word, when the Talmudic teachers themselves, filled with the knowledge of the Lord, were not certain whether their learning and ascetic practices were sufficient to merit reward in the hereafter? How much less could an ordinary Jew expect to enjoy his share of bliss in the world to come, driven as he was from pillar to post in the daily struggle against the ever-stalking specter of starvation, unable to study the Torah or to abide by its multiple requirements? How hopeless the ordinary Jew felt under the circumstances is reflected in the following anecdote:

A traveling peddler was caught in a blizzard while pursuing his trade. Stumbling through mountainous drifts all day, he finally succeeded by midnight in finding his way to a village, where only one house was still lit. It turned out to be the house of the rabbi, who, as was his habit, had studied far into the night. The rabbi received the peddler hospitably, with offers of hot tea and a comfortable lodging. But, now that his physical needs were no longer pressing, the peddler sensed his spiritual perplexity and inquired of his kind host whether, lacking the pleasures of this world, he, wretch that he was, would at least enjoy the delights of the hereafter. The rabbi, conscious of the mountainous burden of demands that were built up by a host of casuists, replied with this remark: "You labor so hard for the things of this world, which nevertheless elude you—how then can you expect to share in the bliss of the hereafter for which you labor not at all?"

Thus, the harassed masses of Jewry saw themselves deprived of all consolations, with the redemption of the Messiah looming in the far distance and the bliss of the hereafter dependent on gifts of talent and luxury of leisure that were not available to them. The very maturity of the Jewish faith, which led it to esteem so highly the exercise of intellectual disciplines, made its compensations seem remote and unreal to those who hungered most passionately for the bread-and-butter consolations of popular faith.

The hour was deeply in need of a man who could redeem Judaism from its dry legalism, and the people from their many fears, ignorance, and strong feeling of abandonment, rejection, and worthlessness. It was a time for a man to relate the people to their God, and bring dignity and self-respect into their lives.

Each generation, it is said, produces its leader. The leader for this generation came forth. His name was Israel. His name, even today, stirs the hearts of all those who are familiar with the history of that particular period. Who was this man, Israel? What gifts did he possess that qualified him to lead his people, to be their voice, their true representative?

ISRAEL'S BACKGROUND

There does not exist a detailed description of the life of Israel. Most of the information that we do have about him has been handed down orally from one generation to the next. All the flimsy sketches relating to his early life, however, seem to agree that Israel was born in Poland in the year 1700, at Okopy, a small town situated on the border of Podolia and Moldavia.

Israel's parents died when he was a very young child and, having been left without any means of support, he was cared for by the community. When Israel grew older, he became an assistant teacher. His duties, however, were not primarily to teach, but to bring the children to school and return them to their homes. Through this task, he won the hearts of the youngsters by his friendliness, and through the sacred songs and prayers he taught them and sang with them as he accompanied them to and from school. Through the children's love for him, he also gained the affection of their parents. The reputation which he established among the young and the old gave him after a while the position of assistant beadle in the synagogue of his community. At night, after his chores were done, he would remain in the synagogue for many hours studying the *Zohar*, the book embodying the teachings of *Kabbalah* (Jewish Mysticism) which was popular at that time. Hardly anyone suspected that this man, who was branded by the rabbis as lazy and an ignoramus, would someday be remembered as one of the great leaders and saints of his people.

At the age of fifteen, he married; but his wife died soon after. Upon remarrying, he left his native town and went to live in a small town near Brody in Eastern Galicia. He chose as his home a hamlet on the fringes of the Carpathian Mountains. Here, he at first sold lime to the people of the surrounding villages, but as his earnings were meager, he became an innkeeper in a village on the banks of the Prut. Still later, he moved to Tlust, a larger town in Galicia, and again occupied himself as a teacher.

It seems that Israel's wanderings from place to place were not a search for material success. He was actually in search of himself. His mind and heart were occupied with thoughts and ideas which sought expression, and could only organize themselves in the proper order, in unity and harmony, in the right place.

It was in nature that Israel found himself. Trees, flowers, birds, mountains, rivers, and lakes fascinated him. In the midst of nature, Israel learned more about himself, man, God, and the universe than any teacher or library of books could reveal to him. Nature prepared Israel for the task with which his life was to be intertwined, the leadership he was to assume among his people, and the lessons he was to impart to them at a later date.

Israel was destined to represent, to guide, and lead the generation of his time, especially the people in whose midst he grew up and developed, whose needs he sensed and whose hearts he understood. The character of Israel, his personality, all that he stood for and represented qualified him for leadership. Though he was not a great scholar, ordinarily a first requisite for Jewish leadership in his day, and although he penned no books and was no great orator, nevertheless there was something about him that singled him out as a genuine human being, as a true son of God.

It sometimes happens that a leader is ahead of his time. In the case of Israel, he was of his period, of the people and for the people, who referred to him as the Ba-al Shem Tov, "Master of the Good Name."

THE TEACHINGS OF THE BA-AL SHEM

Hasidism and the Ba-al Shem are practically synonymous. The man and the movement are one and the same. Hasidism is what the Ba-al Shem propounded, what he taught about God, man, prayer, sin, and community.

THE BA-AL SHEM'S ATTITUDE TOWARD MAN

The rabbis in the day of the Ba-al Shem were arrogant and looked upon the ignorant and the worker with contempt. In the eyes of the Ba-al Shem all were children of God, all were created in His image, all had the Divine spark in them. Thus he walked among the poor, sympathized with them, brought cheer into their hearts. By his love and compassion he lifted the sinner and the rejected to a higher level of morality. When he was criticized for mingling with every low type, his answer was: "Whoever desires to pull his friend out of the mire must be willing to step into it himself." The Ba-al Shem had an unalterable faith in all men, under all conditions and circumstances. "He who loves God," he said, "loves all creatures."

THE BA-AL SHEM'S OBSERVATIONS ON GOD

The Ba-al Shem found God's presence in every animate as well as inanimate thing. All created things, he held, and every product of human intelligence owe their being to God. All generation and all existence spring from the thought and will of God. It is incumbent upon man to believe that all things are pervaded by the divine life. There is nothing that is void of God. God is to be found in the grand manifestations of nature—in the rolling thunder, in the flash of lightning, in the snow-clad mountains, in the mighty trees of the forest, as well as in the humblest flower or blade of grass. He is in the simple and unaffected heart of the ignorant peasant as in the wisdom and learning of the scholar.

"It is necessary," he declared, "for man always to bear in mind that God is with him always and everywhere, that He is the master of all that happens in the universe. Let man realize that, when he looks at things material, he beholds in reality the Divine Countenance, which is present everywhere. Keeping this in mind, man will find it possible to serve the Lord in all things, even in trifles."

ON SIN

The Ba-al Shem viewed sin and infirmity in a very different light from that of the ordinary rabbi. No sin, he taught, so separates us from God that we need despair of return. "Sin," he said, "is not to be despised but purified; not to be fled from, but subordinated. Love and tolerance will restore the most hardened sinner to the path of virtue and goodness." To a father who came to Israel to consult him as to what to do with his son who had strayed from God and the Torah, his reply was, "Love him all the more."

ON PRAYER

The Ba-al Shem broke through the fences of the rabbis, who established the hours of divine worship as well as the places for worship. According to the Ba-al Shem, it is not a man's prayer or the place and time of his uttering it that is important, but the thought and intention that accompany his prayer. When the Ba-al Shem was reproached for praying long after the appointed time for divine worship, he replied, "Can a child be told when he may approach his father?" And, for one who deeply felt the need to pray but did not know how, Israel pointed to the way as indicated in this story:

A poor village Jew was in the habit of worshipping during the Holy Days in Rabbi Israel's synagogue. He had a slow-witted son who did not master the letters of the Aleph Beth (alphabet); hence his father would not take him to the synagogue. But when the boy became thirteen he was allowed to accompany his father to the House of God on Yom Kippur, the Day of Atonement. The boy took a reed and made himself a flute. When the congregation chanted the prayers, he asked his father to allow him to play upon it, but he was forbidden to do so. When the *Neilah*, the closing service of the day, came, the atmosphere in the synagogue grew tense and warm and the hearts of the worshippers melted like candles in their clay sockets. The boy could no longer contain himself and, taking out the flute, he sang and played upon it. The whole congregation stood terrified by the desecration of the service, but Rabbi Israel was happy and called out: "The cloud is pierced and broken, and the power of the Evil One is shattered."

If a Jew was disturbed because he could not concentrate properly on his prayers, due to his poverty, or inability to comprehend the full meaning of his prayers, or if he was guilt-stricken because he had to shorten his prayers during divine worship, as he had to be at the market place at a certain hour, he found comfort in this story the Ba-al Shem once told his followers:

In the same house there once lived a Talmudic scholar and a simple Jewish workman. Both arose very early every morning. The scholar went to the prayer-house and the workman to his toil. The scholar sat in the prayer-house for hours studying the Holy Books and praying until the dinner hour. And then, well satisfied with the fulfillment of his duties to God, he returned home. On his way he met his neighbor returning tired and exhausted from his work; the workman had only a few minutes in which he could go to the prayer-house and say his morning prayers. The Talmudic scholar looked at him with contempt and thought of the great difference between them—he studying so hard and so long in the Holy Books and praying so diligently, while this simple man had been busy all morning with coarse work and had only just said his morning prayers. The workman sighed, fearing for himself when he looked upon his neighbor the Talmudic scholar, who had left the house early in the morning, at the same time as he, and had all these hours been occupied only with holy things, whilst he had been at his hard work.

Weeks, months, and years passed in this way. The Talmudic scholar died, and not long after the workman died too. The scholar was called before the heavenly Judge: "What hast thou done during thy life?" he was asked. "I spent my life in the study of the Talmud and in prayer," he replied. "I observed all the laws to the smallest detail." And he stood back well satisfied. "He despised his neighbor, the workman, who had no time to pray and did not have the knowledge of the Talmud," intervened the celestial counsel. The scales were brought out; all the Talmud studies and the prayers were placed on one side, and on the other his contempt for the workman. And behold! the contempt weighed down the scale on its side and a heavenly voice said: "The Talmudic scholar has no place in Paradise."

Then the workman came up. "What hast thou done during thy life?" he was asked. And he answered with bowed head: "All my life has been spent in hard work. I had to earn my bread by the sweat of my brow to provide for my wife and children, and therefore I had no time to say my prayers properly." "But he always looked enviously towards his neighbor, the Talmudic scholar, sighing and full of humility," intervened the celestial counsel. And behold! a divine voice cried aloud: "Bring the workman into Paradise."

THE FIVE PRINCIPLES OF HASIDISM

The teachings of the Ba-al Shem are embodied in five main principles, and these are the foundation of Hasidism.

HUMILITY

The first is "Humility." Humility, according to the Ba-al Shem, is expressed by thinking highly of one's neighbor and humbly of oneself. The true lover of God, he preached, is also the lover of man. It is ignorance of one's errors that makes one ready to see the errors of others. Humility is one's awareness of his own foibles, weaknesses, temptations, and fallibility, and the viewing of the faults of others with sympathy, kindliness, and compassion. He is truly humble who feels for the other as for himself and sees in himself the other. Humility is an antidote to haughtiness. The haughty man is not he who knows himself, but he who compares himself with others. The arrogant man sits in judgment over those faults in others by which he himself is identified.

CHEERFULNESS

The second principle of Hasidism is "Cheerfulness." Judaism advocates a happy attitude toward life; God is to be served with a smile, so to speak, as the Psalmist said, "Serve the Lord with gladness," and as the Talmud suggests, "The Schekinah, the Divine Presence, rests upon a person, not when he is sad, depressed, but only when he is joyous in the awareness of doing the will of God."

These lessons on how to face life, on how to serve God, taught by Judaism for centuries, had to be taught once again to the depressed Jews of Eastern Europe. Their hard life and lot forced them to forget how to live and how to laugh. Cheerfulness was therefore regarded as a supreme virtue in the teachings of the Ba-al Shem. "Even if one has stumbled into sin," said Israel, "he should not give way to sadness, which negates the value of anything he might do, but let him confine his regrets to the sinful act and return in joy to the service of the Creator."

ENTHUSIASM

The third principle of Hasidism is "Enthusiasm." Enthusiasm, in the view of Hasidism, is an outpouring of love. It is an expression of the best self through action. Enthusiasm is infectious; it touches hearts and links hands to create, to build, to overcome obstacles, to enrich, and to ennoble. Enthusiasm brings heaven closer to earth and lifts the earthly heavenward. Enthusiasm marches forward. It sees a bright day, a bright world ahead. Enthusiasm is courage, confidence, and faith combined.

INTENTION

The fourth cardinal principle of Hasidism is "Intention." Intention may be described as intensity of feeling or absorption. This means that whatever act one is performing, be it religious or mundane, one must throw himself into it with his whole heart and soul. According to Hasidism there is no line of demarcation between the sacred and the profane. Whatever is said and done in the name of God is sanctified.

UNION

The fifth basic principle of Hasidism is "Union." According to this principle the gulf between the individual and God must be closed. Man is separated from God by his concentration on the material life, but his longing is to unite with the Godhead. By de-emphasizing the importance of things material, man's soul is liberated, flows into the Infinite, and thus union with the Godhead is attained.

Through his love, piety, humility, cheerfulness, enthusiasm, and understanding, Ba-al Shem succeeded in lifting a large portion of his depressed brethren from the depths of despair, giving them fresh hope, a healthy outlook on life and uniting them into a community of fellowship.

ON COMMUNITY

Hasidism taught that each person was needed by his brother, for each, according to the Master, was unique; and the uniqueness of each was necessary to the welfare and happiness of the whole community. How important each was to the whole, the Ba-al Shem told his followers in this parable:

"Some men stood under a very high tree. And one of the men saw that in the top of the tree stood a bird, glorious with genuine beauty. A great longing came over the man to reach the bird and take it. But because of the height of the tree this was not in his power, and a ladder was not to be found. Still, out of his great and powerful longing he found a way. He took the men who stood around him and placed them on top of one another, each on the shoulder of a comrade. He, however, climbed to the top so that he reached the bird and took it. And although the men had helped him, they knew nothing of the bird and did not see it. But he, who knew and saw it, would not have been able to reach it without them. If, moreover, the lowest of them had left his place, then those above him would have fallen to the earth."

After his death, in 1760, the Ba-al Shem was succeeded by such men as Rabbi Baer of Meseritz, Rabbi Jacob Joseph of Polona, Rabbi Levi Yitzhok of Berditchev, Rabbi Nahum of Tchernobyl, Rabbi Schneur Salomon of Ladi, Rabbi Nahman of Bratzlav, and a number of others who caught his spirit and were worthy of leadership; but the first blush of the movement went with the passing of its founder.

CONCLUSION

Both Jew and Judaism benefited by the life of the Ba-al Shem. Both were revitalized, both were strengthened.

Even for our own day, the lessons of Hasidism have much to offer. If one were to take its doctrines seriously, it would open his eyes unto himself and unto the world, and show him how he could best serve both.

7. A Time Without God

For nearly two thousand years the life of Western man was shaped, formed, and governed by the Judaeo-Christian ethic. Each generation transmitted this ethic to the next. Few found fault with it or dared question its validity. Anyone who did, faced the wrath of the community in which he lived. Under this system, one was provided with the answers to the questions of what was right or wrong, good or evil. If one secretly deviated from any of the accepted, approved, time-honored principles which he was expected to follow, he was plagued by a feeling of guilt from which he was relieved either by penance, prayer, charity, or all of these combined.

The Judaeo-Christian ethic was man's highest authority. It was taught by parents, elaborated by the clergy, repeated by teachers, stressed by officials of the State, all of whom were respected, honored, and obeyed. After all, they were the purveyor's of God's will. To live in accordance with God's will meant for most people not only to win the love of one's neighbor, but particularly God's favor, which they believed would guarantee them a place in heaven.

The Judaeo-Christian ethic offered man meaning and direction for his life; it created a certain orderliness, steadiness, and stability in society. This is not to say that crime of one sort or another was completely unknown. Society was never free of the thief, the scoundrel, the murderer. But, because social approval for one's conduct was so deeply coveted, acts of a forbidden nature were generally avoided and therefore rare.

This manner of life slowly but surely began to erode beginning with the Industrial Revolution in the eighteenth century, and the pace of its deterioration rapidly increased following the development of science and technology in the nineteenth century, and especially soon after World War II. Both the Industrial Revolution and science wrought radical changes in every aspect of life. It affected religion, education, politics, government, philosophy, and numerous other aspects of human thought and conduct. Communal life was undermined, old beliefs no longer received the allegiance of past generations, individualism began to replace institutionalism, and secularism that of the sacred.

The various cultural changes culminated in declaring God as dead in the Sixties of our century. Although Friedrich Nietzsche, the German philosopher (1844-1900), wrote of the death of God about one hundred years before, at that time Western man was not as yet fully ready either to fathom the meaning of Nietzsche's statement concerning God or to accept the idea with any seriousness. As a matter of fact, Nietzsche was blasted by the Church for such a blasphemous, outrageous reference to the Supreme Being. In our day, however, when books or articles appear on the "Death of God," not too many are shaken by such references. Why?

While Western man does not deny the value of the basic principles of the Judaeo-Christian ethic, yet his daily conduct shows little evidence, if any, of their influence on him. Thus, it is not too difficult for him at this point in time to comprehend that the reference to God's death is really an allusion to himself. Now he understands it to mean, not that God is dead, but that God is dead in him.

Even those who in one way or another are involved in the Church, attend regularly the weekly service, and want to live in accordance with God's commandments, experience an inner struggle. For our materialistically oriented culture indicates to them every day, in numerous instances, that profit and religion do not easily mix; that business and religion are diametrically opposed to each other; that a society which is consumed by things gives little thought to spirituality, leaves no room for God.

Now, without God, whom man for thousands of years regarded as his light and guide, each person needs to find his own way, create his own morality, his own values. Since only a few are capable of doing so, our society is therefore beset with chaos, crime, and confusion. Parents are at a loss as to what spiritual lessons they can honestly impart to their children. The Church has been rendered ineffective as a teacher. The community as an agent of influence is practically powerless since each of its members is on his own with no common denominator to hold them together. The school, which used to reiterate the teachings in the home, does not know what the home represents anymore, and the same is true of the State.

Living in this kind of an atmosphere, in a society with God no longer controlling man's destiny, the present generation may be said to be disoriented. It has little, if anything, to identify with; it is totally uprooted, cut off from the past, and lacks a sense of continuity and unity. Its members feel abandoned, anguished, bewildered, despondent, and lonely. Their cry, "Who am I?" is a graphic reflection of their condition of disorientedness.

"Although," says Leroy F. Troutner, "one can find sprinkled

throughout history those few perceptive poets and seers who have asked the question 'Who am I?' never before has a whole generation chorused this concern. The reason for this, I believe, is that in the past man in a vague, average sort of way has been aware of an identity. In his transcendence he has always been able to identify with something larger than himself. For one thing he could identify with the natural environment of earth, air, water, and sky. It was larger than man, and besides, he lived in and through this environment. Not only could man identify with the natural world, but he could also find himself in the supernatural world of the Christian-Judaic God.... Modern man no longer has an obvious and easy object or myth of identification to provide the increasingly sought answer to who he is."[62]

This explains why some in our society turn to the culture of the East, hoping to discover there an ideal for their vacuous, directionless lives, or experiment with drugs, imagining that these will offer them the religious experience they yearn for, or join cults for identification and solace. And others, failing in their search, choose suicide as the answer to their troubled, restive souls.

Until Western man rediscovers transcendency—that is, a power, a force, greater than himself, perhaps a new God concept—he will remain without identity. Not until he becomes aware that the ingredient his soul is deeply in need of is that of spirituality will he know rest.

It is through man's spiritual life that a bond is created between him and his fellow men, that order is established in society, that direction, meaning, and purpose for one's life is obtained.

---

[62] See "The Confrontation Between Experimentalism and Existentialism," by Leroy F. Troutner, in *Philosophy for a New Generation*, Roger Eastman, ed. (New York: The Macmillan Co., 1970), p. 75.

Bibliography
Part I

PHILOSOPHY

Aristotle. *The Nichomachean Ethics* (Cambridge: Harvard University Press, 1968).

Ascoli, Max. *The Power of Freedom* (New York: Farrar Strauss, 1949).

Ayer, A.J. ed. *The Humanist Outlook* (London: Pemberton, 1968).

Barrett, William. *What is Existentialism?* (New York: Grove Press, 1964).

Berdyaev, Nicolas. *The Destiny of Man* (New York: Harper Brothers, 1960).

Blackham, H.J. *Humanism* (Hamondsworth, England: Penguin Books, 1968).

Bode, Boyd. *Democracy a Way of Life* (New York: The Macmillan Co., 1943).

Bonhoeffer, Dietrich. *Ethics* (New York: The Macmillan Co., 1958).

Boronowski, J. *The Identity of Man*, rev. ed. (Garden City, N.Y.: Doubleday, 1971).

Bradley, F.H. *Ethical Studies* (New York: Liberal Arts Press, 1947).

Britton, Karl. *Philosophy and Meaning of Life* (Cambridge: Cambridge University Press, 1969).

Clarke, Arthur C. *Profiles of the Future* (New York: Bantam, 1964).

Cubberley, E.P. *A History of Education* (Boston: Houghton Mifflin Co., 1920).

Dewey, John. *Democracy and Education* (New York: The Macmillan Co., 1916).

——. *Human Nature and Conduct* (New York: Henry Holt and Co., 1947).

Dole, Charles F. *The Ethics of Progress*, (New York: Thomas Y. Crowell and Co., 1909).

Heinemann, F.H. *Existentialism and the Modern Predicament* (New York: Harper Brothers, 1958).

Heschel, Abraham J. *Who is Man?* (Stanford, Calif.: Stanford University Press, 1965).

Hocking, W.E. *Human Nature and Its Remaking* (New Haven: Yale University Press, 1932).

——. *Man and the State* (Oxford: Oxford University Press, 1926).

Jaeger, Werner W. *Humanism and Theology* (Milwaukee: Marquette University Press, 1967).

Jasper, Karl. *Man in the Modern Age*, trans. by Eden and Cedar Paul (New York: Doubleday, Anchor Books, 1951).

Kahn, Herman. *The Year 2,000* (New York: The Macmillan Co., 1967).

Kaplan, Abraham. *The New World of Philosophy* (New York: Vintage Books, Random House, 1961).

Lamont, Corliss. *The Philosophy of Humanism* (New York: Ungar, 1965).

Leiser, Burton M. *Liberty, Justice, and Morals* (New York: The Macmillan Co., 1973).

Macquarrie, John. *Existentialism* (New York: Penguin Books, 1972).

Marcel, Gabriel. *Philosophy of Existentialism* (New York: Citadel, 1961).

May, Rollo. *Man's Search of Himself* (New York: Dell, 1961).

Mead, Shepherd. *How to Get to the Future before It Gets to You* (New York: Hawthorn, 1974).

Monroe, Paul. *Textbook in the History of Education* (New York: The Macmillan Co., 1905).

Montague, Ashley. *The Direction of Human Development* (New York: Hawthorn Books, 1970).

Mouat, Kit. *What Humanism is About* (London: Barrie Books, 1963).

Muirhead, J.H. *Elements of Ethics* (New York: Charles Scribner's Sons, 1932).

Newman, Franz L. *Democratic and Authoritarian State: Essay in Political and Legal Theory* (New York: Free Press, 1957).

Oppenheimer, Franz. *The State*, trans. by John M. Gitterman, (New York: The Bobbs-Merrill Co., 1914).

Ostrovsky, Everett. *Self Discovery and Social Awareness* (New York: Wiley, 1974).

Patka, Frederick. *Existentialist Thinkers and Thoughts* (New York: Philosophical Library, 1962).

Paton, H.J. *The Good Will* (New York: The Macmillan Co., 1927).

Rashdall, H. *Is Conscience an Emotion?* (Boston: Houghton Mifflin, 1914).

Reese, Curtiss W. *The Meaning of Humanism* (Boston, Beacon Press, 1945).

Ross, W.D. *Foundations of Ethics* (Oxford: Oxford University Press, 1939).

Rousseau, Jean Jacques. *The Social Contract* (New York: E.P. Dutton, 1950).

Royce, Josiah. *The World and the Individual* (New York: The Macmillan Co., 1927).

Sartre, Jean-Paul. *Essays in Existentialism* (New York: Philosophical Library, 1965).

Seth, James. *A Study of Ethical Principles* (New York: Charles Scribner's Sons, 1926).

Stace, W.T. *The Concept of Morals* (New York: The Macmillan Co., 1937).

Tead, Ordway. *The Art of Leadership* (New York: McGraw-Hill Co., Inc., 1935).

Wahl, Jean. *A Short History of Existentialism* (New York: Philosophical Library, 1952).

Washburn, Carleton W. *A Living Philosophy of Education* (New York: John Day Company, 1940).

Weldon, Thomas D. *State and Morals, The Ethical Basis of the State* (Princeton, N.J.: Princeton University Press, 1924).

West, Ranyard. *Conscience and Society* (London: Methuen, 1942).

Wheelis, Allen. *How People Change* (New York: Harper & Row, 1973).

Whitehead, Alfred North. *Aims of Education* (New York: Mentor, 1960).

Part II

RELIGION

Altizer, Thomas J.J., and Hamilton, William. *Radical Theology and the Death of God* (New York: Bobbs-Merrill, 1966).

Bacon, T.S. *The Beginnings of Religion*, an essay (London, 1887).

Benham, William. *The Dictionary of Religion* (London, 1887).

Briggs, William S., ed. *Anthology of Zen* (New York: Grove Press, 1961).

Buber, Martin. *Hasidism and Modern Man*, ed. and translated by Maurice Friedman (Horizon Press, 1958).

———. *Hasidism* (New York: Philosophical Library, 1948).

Chinmor, Sri. *Yoga and Spiritual Life* (New York: Aum Publications, 1974).

Cook, F.G. *The Origin of Religion and Language*, considered in five essays (London, 1884).

Danielou, Alain. *Yoga: Method of Reintegration* (New York: University Books, 1949).

DeBary, W. Theodore, ed. *Sources of Indian Tradition* (New York: Columbia University Press, 1958).

Eliade, Mircea. *Yoga: Immortality and Freedom* (Princeton, N.J.: Princeton University Press, 1970).

Fromm, Erich. *Zen Buddhism and Psychoanalysis* (New York: Harper & Row, 1970).

Herman, E. *The Meaning and Value of Mysticism* (London, 1915).

Horodezky, A.S. *Leaders of Hasidism*, trans. by Marcia Horodezky (London: Hasefer for Literature, 1928).

Ice, Jackson L., and Carey John J., eds. *Death of God Debate* (Philadelphia: Westminster Press, 1965).

Inge, William R. *Studies of English Mystics* (Plainview, N.Y.: Books for Libraries, 1906).

James, William. *Varieties of Religious Experience* (New York: The Modern Library, Random House, 1902).

———. *Essays on Faith and Morals* (New York: Longman's Green and Co., 1947).

Jastrow, Morris. *The Study of Religion* (London: The Walter Scott Publishing Co., 1901).

John of the Cross, Saint. *The Ascent of Mount Carmel*, trans. by David Lewis, new edition (London, 1906).

Jones, Rufus. *The Flowering of Mysticism* (New York: Hafner Publishing Co., 1971).

———. *Studies in Mystical Religion* (London: The Macmillan Co., 1923).

Kahana, A. *Sefer Ha-Hasiduth* (Warsaw, 1922).

Kellogg, S.H. *Genesis and Growth of Religion* (New York: 1892).

Minkin, Jacob S. *The Romance of Hasidism* (New York: The Macmillan Co., 1935).

Newman, Louis, I. *The Hasidic Anthology* (New York: Charles Scribner's Sons, 1935).

Otto, Rudolph. *Mysticism East and West* (Oxford: Oxford University Press, 1924).

Plotinus. *The Enneads*, trans. by Stephen McKenna (London, 1917).

Radhakrishnan, S. *The Hindu View of Life* (London, 1931).

Schecter, Solomon. *Studies in Judaism*, see essay "The Chassidim" (Philadelphia: Jewish Publication Society of America, reprinted 1945).

Scholem, Gershom. *Major Trends in Jewish Mysticism* (Jerusalem: Schocken Publishing House, 1941).

Spencer, Sidney. *Mysticism in World Religion* (New York: A.S. Barnes & Co., 1963).

Stace, W.T. *Mysticism and Philosophy* (Philadelphia: Lippincott, 1960).

Suzuki, Daisetz T. *Essays in Zen Buddhism* (London: Luzac, 1934).

Tiele, C.P. *Outlines of the History of Religions*, trans. from the Dutch by J.E. Carpenter (London, 1887).

Underhill, Evelyn. *Mysticism* (New York: E.P. Dutton, 1911).

Vahanian, Gabriel. *The Death of God* (New York: Braziller, 1964).

Walker, Benjamin. *The Hindu World—an Encyclopedic Survey of Hinduism* (New York: Praeger Publishers, 1968).

Watkin, Edward I. *The Philosophy of Mysticism* (London: Grant Richards, 1920).

Watts, Alan W. *The Way of Zen* (New York: Pantheon Books, 1957).

Weisel, Elie. *Souls on Fire* (New York: Vintage Books, 1973).

Index

A

Adam, 43
Allegory, 137
Aphrodite, 127
Apollo, 127
Aristippus, 109
Aristotle, 3
Arnold, Matthew, 114
Augustine, Saint, 44

B

Ba-al Shem Tov, 159
Benevolence, 103
Berdyaev, Nicolas, 88
Bergson, Henri, 45, 132

Bhakti Yoga, 150
Brahman, 153

C

Cheerfulness, 163
Community, 165
Conformity, 50
Conscience, 98
Consciousness, 99
Cooley, Charles H., 52, 63
Cyrenaic, 109

D

Deists, 120
Democracy, 57

177

DATE